MINISTRY OF MUNITIONS.

Technical Department—Aircraft Production.

GOTHA.

I.O. 644.

KINGSWAY,
W.C. 2

REPORT ON
GOTHA BOMBER

With Notes on Giant Aeroplanes.

SEPTEMBER, 1918.

The Naval & Military Press Ltd

Published by
The Naval & Military Press Ltd
5 Riverside, Brambleside, Bellbrook
Industrial Estate, Uckfield, East Sussex,
TN22 1QQ England

Tel: +44 (0) 1825 749494
Fax: +44 (0) 1825 765701

www.naval-military-press.com
www.military-genealogy.com

In reprinting in facsimile from the original, any imperfections are inevitably reproduced and the quality may fall short of modern type and cartographic standards.

MINISTRY OF MUNITIONS.

Technical Department—Aircraft Production.

GOTHA.

I.O. 644.

KINGSWAY,
W.C. 2

REPORT ON
GOTHA BOMBER

With Notes on Giant Aeroplanes.

SEPTEMBER, 1918.

TABLE OF CONTENTS.

Two-Engined Type.

	Page.
Introductory	1
Wing Construction	2
Struts	3
Ailerons	3
Propeller Accommodation	3
Empennage	4
Fuselage	4
Undercarriage	5
Engine Mounting	7
Engines	8
Radiators	8
Exhaust Manifolds	9
Aeroplane Controls	10
Engine Controls	11
Petrol System	11
Armament	12
Bombs	13
Wireless	14
Instruments	14
Fabric and Dope	14
Modifications in Gotha shot down July 4, 1918	14

Four-Engined Giant.

General Description	15
Wing Construction	19
Ailerons	20
Interplane Struts	20
Bracing	20
Tail Unit	20
Elevators	22
Fins	22
Rudders	22
Undercarriage	22
Armament	22
Bomb Gear	22

Five-Engined Giant.

General Description	23

INDEX OF ILLUSTRATIONS.

Fig. No.		Page.
1.	Rib	2
2 and 3.	Spar Sections	2
4.	Upper Wing Spar Joint	3
5 and 5a.	Lower Wing Spar Joint	3
6.	Strut Joint	3
7.	Rear Gunner's Cockpit	4
8.	Rear Gun Tunnel	5
9.	Bracket Joint (Fuselage to Upper Plane)	5
10.	End of Axle	6
11.	Tail Skid	6
12.	Top of Tail Skid	7
13 and 14.	Engine Bearers	7
15.	Ball Joint of Engine Bearer Struts	7
16.	Cross Piece between Engine Bearers	8
17.	Foot of Engine Bearer Support Tube	8
18 and 19.	Radiators, showing Shutters	8
20.	Shutter Control	9
21 and 22.	Exhaust Manifolds	9
23 and 24.	Aileron Control Details	10
25.	Rudder Cranks	10
26.	Throttle Levers	11
27.	Dashboard	11
28.	Control Tap	11
29, 30, and 31.	Forward Gun Mounting	12
32 and 33.	Bomb Carrier Details	13
34.	Bomber's Cockpit	13
35.	Aileron Modification	14
36 and 37.	Rudder Control (Modification)	15
38.	Engine Mounting (Four-Engined Type)	15
39.	General Arrangement Drawings (Four-Engined Type)	16
40 and 41.	General Arrangement Drawings (Four-Engined Type)	17
42.	Probable Construction (Four-Engined Type)	18
43.	Spar Sections (Four-Engined Type)	19
44.	Rib (Four-Engined Type)	20
45.	Rudder	21
46.	Engine Bearers (Five-Engined Type)	24
47.	Tail Skid (Five-Engined Type)	25
48—50.	Biplane Tail (Two-Engined Type)	26
51.	Flywheel and Clutch (Four-Engined Type)	27
52.	Gear Box and Radiator (Four-Engined Type)	27
53.	Radiator (Four-Engined Type)	27
54.	Gear Box and Shaft (Four-Engined Type)	28
55.	Empennage (Four-Engined Type)	28
56.	Empennage (Four-Engined Type)	29
57.	Undercarriage (Four-Engined Type)	29
58.	Axles and Wheels (Four-Engined Type)	29
59.	Photograph of Wreckage (Four-Engined Type)	30
60.	Rear of Fuselage (Four-Engined Type)	30
61.	Power Plant (Four-Engined Type)	30
62.	Main Planes and Ailerons (Four-Engined Type)	31
63.	Strut and Compression Tube (Four Engined Type)	31
64.	Bomb Carrier (Four-Engined Type)	31
65.	Photograph of Wreckage (Four-Engined Type)	32
66.	Long Gear Box and Clutch (Five-Engined Type)	32
67.	Long Gear Box (from beneath) (Five-Engined Type)	32
68.	Long Gear Box and Oil Radiator (Five-Engined Type)	33
69.	Driving Pinion (Five-Engined Type)	33
70.	Windmill (Five-Engined Type)	33
71.	Oil Radiator and Gear Pump (Five-Engined Type)	34
72.	Pusher Screw and Pinion (Five-Engined Type)	34
73.	Tractor Screw and Pinion (Five-Engined Type)	34
74.	Gear Box Oil Filter (Five-Engined Type)	35
75.	Engine Controls (Five-Engined Type)	35
76.	Transverse Girder of Engine Bearers (Five-Engined Type)	35
77.	"Douglas" Type Power Unit for Wireless (Five-Engined Type)	35
78.	Pump and Transformer (Five-Engined Type)	36
79.	Engine and Flywheel (Five-Engined Type)	36
80.	Wireless Generator (Five-Engined Type)	36
81.	Cowling and Dynamo Drive (Five-Engined Type)	36
82.	Front of Two-Engined Fuselage	36
	Two-Engined Undercarriage (scale drawing, General Arrangement of Two-Engined Type)	at end.

REPORT

ON

GOTHA BOMBER

WITH NOTES ON GIANT AEROPLANES.

This machine is now on view at the Enemy Aircraft View Room, Agricultural Hall, Islington. Passes can be obtained upon application to Ap. D. (L.), Pen Corner House, Kingsway, W.C. 2.

The standard type of two-engine Gotha is a pusher, the appearance of which is characterised by the backward sweep of the main planes, which are also set at a lateral dihedral angle.

The set back of the planes is 4 deg., and the dihedral approximately 2 deg.

The following are the principal dimensions of the aeroplane, of which general arrangement drawings are given at the end of the report:—

Maximum span	77 ft.
Span of lower plane	71 ft. 9 in.
Gap	7 ft.
Maximum chord	7 ft. 6 in.
Minimum chord	7 ft. 2½ in.
Over-all length	41 ft.
Area of top plane	521.6 sq. ft.
Area of bottom plane	464 sq. ft.
Total area	985 sq. ft.
Area of upper aileron	32 sq. ft.
Area of balance of aileron	3.2 sq. ft.
Area of bottom aileron	22.4 sq. ft.
Span of tail planes	13 ft. 6 in.
Area of tail planes	45 sq. ft.
Area of rudder	16 sq. ft.
Area of rudder balance	3.2 sq. ft.
Area of elevators	19.2 sq. ft.
Area of fin	11.2 sq. ft.
Area of body in horizontal plane	96 sq. ft.
Area of body in vertical plane	107 sq. ft.
Weight empty	2,740 kg. = 6,039 lbs.
Useful load	1,235 kg. = 2,722 lbs.
Total weight fully loaded	3,975 kg. = 8,763 lbs.
Loading per sq. ft.	8.9 lbs.

ENGINES.

Two 260 H.P. Mercedes.

Engine centres	14 ft.
Propeller diameter	10 ft. 2 in.
Track of main landing wheels	3 ft. 2½ in.
Track of auxiliary landing wheels	2 ft. 7½ in.

The speed of this machine at 12,000 ft. is estimated at 72 miles per hour.

CONSTRUCTION.

Wings.—The wings of this aeroplane are of wooden construction throughout, and have a section as shown in Fig. 1. This drawing also illustrates the construction of the rib (the web of which is of three-ply wood, extensively perforated, and the flange of solid wood

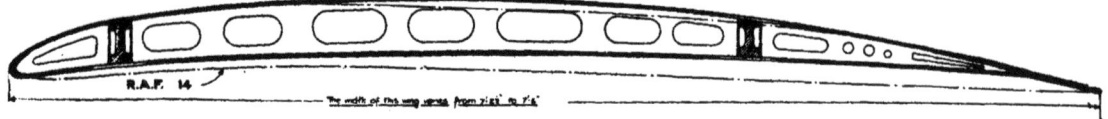

Fig. 1.

grooved to fit upon the web, to which it is tacked).

For the purposes of comparison, the section of the R.A.F. 14 wing is super-imposed and drawn to the same scale. This is shown in broken lines.

The disposal of the spars is as follows:—

Leading edge to centre of leading spar, 9 in.

Centre of leading spar to centre of trailing spar, 4 ft. 4 in.

Centre of trailing spar to trailing edge, 2 ft. 5 in.

The space between the leading edge and the leading spar is covered as to the upper surface with three-ply, the rest of the wing being covered with fabric in the usual way.

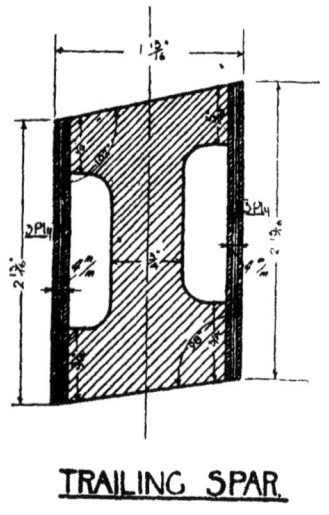

TRAILING SPAR

Fig. 2.

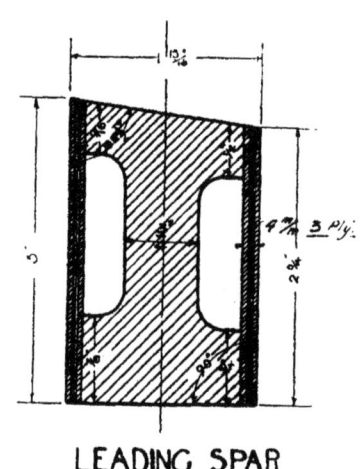

LEADING SPAR

Fig. 3.

The spars possess several points of interest, and their dimensions and method of construction are presented in Figs. 2 and 3, from which it will be seen that they differ from the practice adopted in other German designs.

The I Section main members are of spruce. The three-ply walls, applied to them by glueing and tacking, are principally birch, and are 4 mm. thick.

The spars are wrapped with fabric throughout.

In the earlier Gotha designs the sweep back of the wings was 10 deg. In the present design it is 4 deg., due probably to the fact that other means have been successfully adopted to get the centre of gravity sufficiently forward.

It will be seen from the scale drawings that whereas the upper wing surface consists of two portions which unite at the centre line of the machine, the lower plane on each side consists of the centre section attached to the base of the fuselage, and an outward extension, between which is interposed a short span of plane forming, with the engine bearers and their struts, and the landing carriages on each side, a completely independent and separate unit. These small sections of planes are covered in with three-ply, both top and bottom, and the same material is used for the upper surface of the centre section of the lower plane.

At the junction of the two upper wings, a rather unusual joint is employed; this is illustrated in Fig. 4, and consists of a series of rectangular staples which are held together by a steel wedge. The joints used in the lower plane are of a different character, and embody the usual pin principle, giving the spars, when not braced by the wiring, a hingeing action in the vertical plane. This joint is shown in Fig. 5, which also illustrates the manner in which the wings are braced against drag stresses by means of very light steel compression tubes and cables.

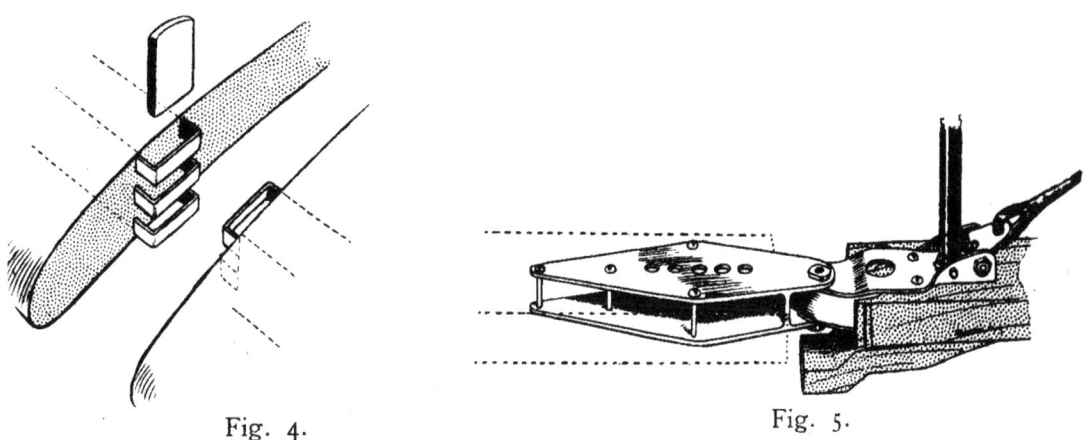

Fig. 4.   Fig. 5.

Another view of the box joint on the spar end is given in Fig. 5a, which shows its internal construction. Joints of the above design are used on either side of the engine bearer section.

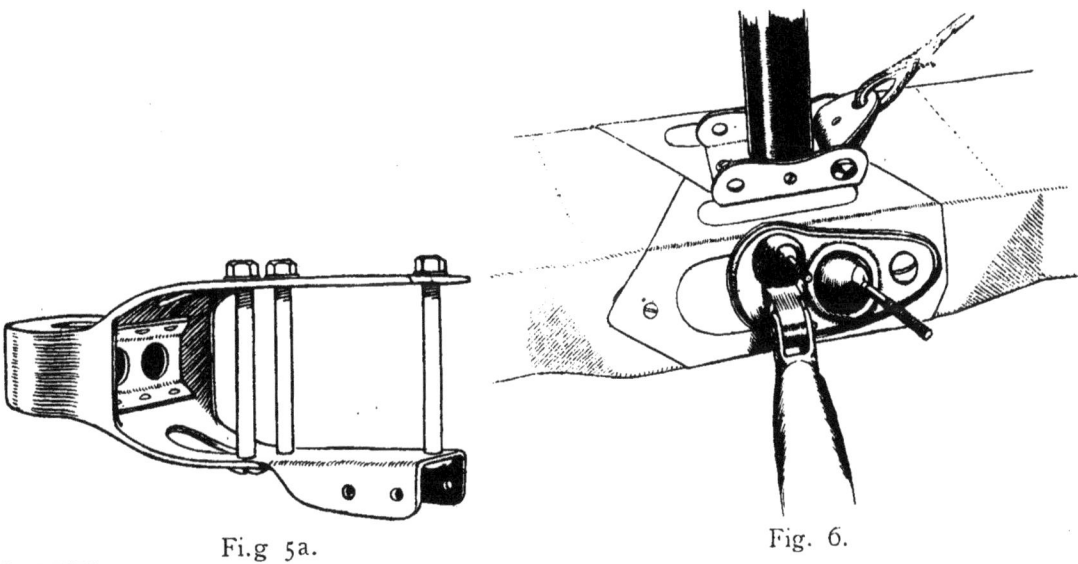

Fi.g 5a.   Fig. 6.

STRUTS.

Apart from the struts which separate the engine eggs and brace them to the fuselage, there are three pairs of interplane struts on each wing. These struts are composed of steel tubing to which is attached a three-ply fairing. The design of the strut joint is shown in Fig. 6.

The wire bracing throughout is by multi-strand steel cable, the fitting of which, however, presents no features of interest.

AILERONS.

Only the upper ailerons are balanced, the upper and lower ailerons being connected by a single strut on each side. The operating lever is fitted on the top aileron, and works in a slot cut in the upper main plane. From this lever wires are taken over pulleys on the leading spar of the lower plane, and thence to the fuselage through the space between the leading edge and the forward spar.

Where the wires pass through the small sections of lower plane under the engines, they are provided with detachable connections which can be inspected through hinged flaps.

The framework of the ailerons is of steel tube throughout, involving a welded-up one-piece construction.

PROPELLER ACCOMMODATION.

In order to permit the engine eggs to be placed sufficiently far forward to allow of the centre of gravity being correct, considerable inroads have had to be made in the trailing edge of both upper and lower planes in order to give scope for the propellers. In front of the screws, the chord of the planes is reduced to 5 ft. 9 in., and at this point the trailing edge is very blunt.

EMPENNAGE.

The whole of the empennage construction is of steel tubing, and the various components are rigidly braced together by inclined streamline struts, which, as in the case of the main struts, are of circular section steel tubing, to which a three-ply fairing has been added.

These external struts give the Gotha tail a somewhat clumsy appearance, and would seem furthermore to exercise a notable masking effect upon the rear gun. Only the rudder is balanced, and it will be noticed that the area of this organ, compared with that of the fin, is very large.

FUSELAGE.

The fuselage is in one piece from nose to rudder post, and is an entirely wooden construction, consisting of the usual longerons and wooden transverse members. It is covered in with three-ply throughout its length on the top, bottom and sides, but whereas in most German aeroplanes the three-ply lining is relied upon for solidifying the structure, in this machine it is extensively reinforced by diagonal wire bracings, especially in the forward portion of the fuselage at the point at which the main planes are attached.

In the extreme front is placed the front gunner's cockpit. Immediately behind him, and on the left-hand side of the machine, sits the pilot; beside him is a folding seat for another passenger.

Between the pilot's seat and the rear gunner's cockpit are placed the two main petrol tanks, which occupy the full width of the fuselage.

The original intention of the designer was evidently to fit tanks of smaller capacity, shaped in such a way as to provide a communication tunnel between the pilot's seat and the rear gunner's cockpit. For this purpose the wooden bulkheads on each end of the tank space are deeply cut away on the left-hand side. With the existing arrangement of tanks, however, no interchange of personnel is possible.

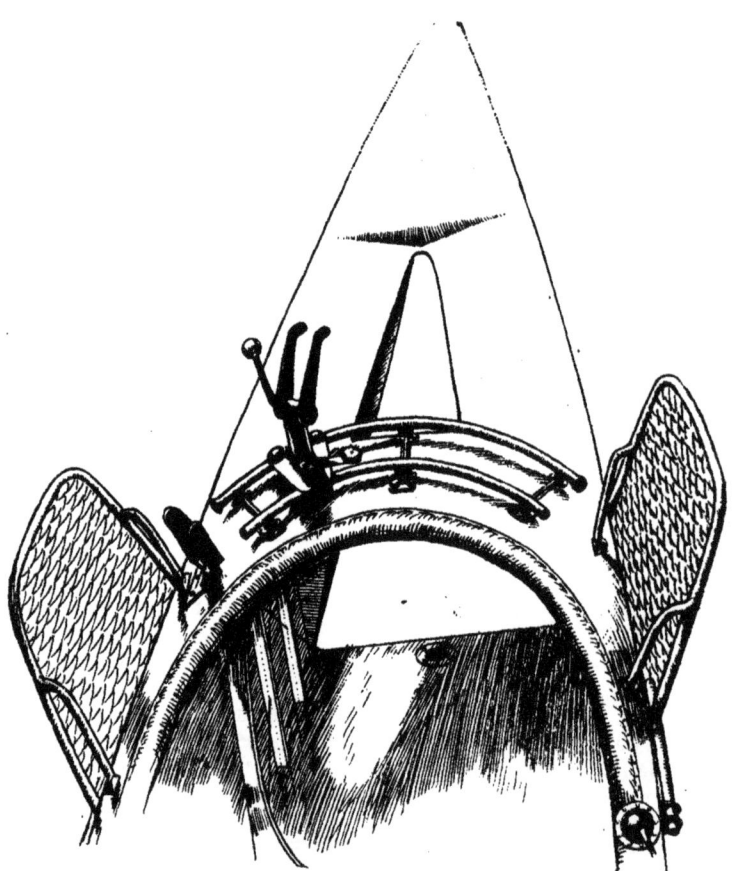

Fig. 7.

Another small point of interest is the inclination of the back of the pilot's seat; for this purpose careful consideration of space has resulted in a wedge-shaped piece being let into the forward tank, indicating again that all possible means have been adopted to get the C.G. sufficiently forward.

The rear tank is of identical construction, and also possesses this wedge-shaped arrangement. In this case, however, the wedge-shaped piece represents waste of space.

The rear gunner's cockpit is roomy and provided with a folding seat. Abaft of it, the fuselage is furnished with an elaborate gun tunnel, which, however, differs very markedly from that which was incorporated in the earlier Gotha designs, in which the fuselage was completely covered in as to its top surface, and the tunnel was only used for a gun mounted on the floor of the cockpit. In the present design, the tunnel is furnished with a V-shaped opening in the upper surface, so that the gun mounted on the top of the fuselage can fire backwards and downwards through an arc of about 25 deg. laterally and about 60 deg. vertically. This is shown in Fig. 7.

The inside of this tunnel is lined with three-ply wood, and its arrangement is clearly shown in Fig. 8. On the floor of the fuselage, in the rear gunner's cockpit, a mount is provided for a second gun, but in none of the Gotha machines brought down was a gun fitted at this point.

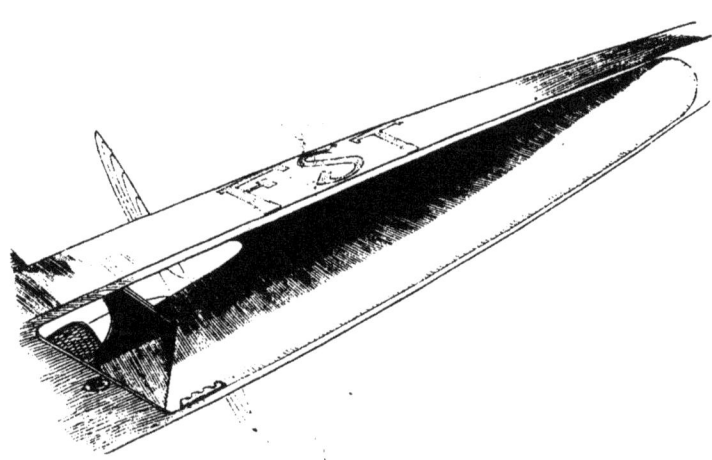

Fig. 8.

It is noted that to give the rear gunner a greater feeling of security, and to prevent any loose articles from falling out, wooden cross pieces are fitted up immediately in front of the tunnel opening. At the forward end of the tunnel the fuselage is evidently weak, as it was at this point that breakage occurred in most of the machines brought down.

Fig. 9 illustrates one of the brackets by means of which the fuselage is secured to the upper main plane; it carries a short stream-lined strut. It will be noticed that the characteristic German dome-shaped clip is used, but that in this case the usual welded joint is replaced

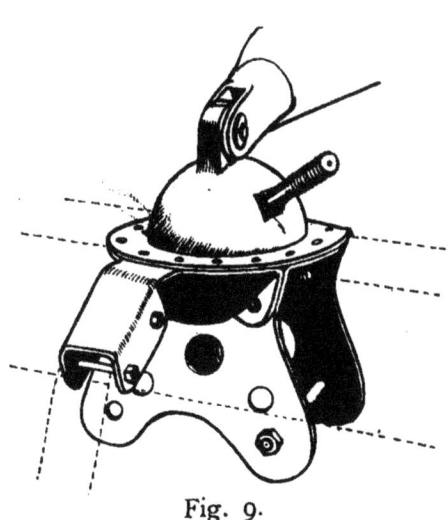

Fig. 9.

by rivets. This bracket occurs at the after bulkhead immediately behind the rear petrol tank; the dotted lines proceeding from the small clip indicate how this bulkhead is cut away so as to provide, in the original scheme, an opening through which the personnel could squeeze in order to change places if necessary.

UNDERCARRIAGE.

The undercarriages on each side form, with the engine mountings and a small section of the lower main plane, completely independent units. There is no landing wheel under the nose of the machine as is the case in the Friedrichschafen design. Each undercarriage has four wheels. The larger pair are attached to an axle placed immediately under the centre

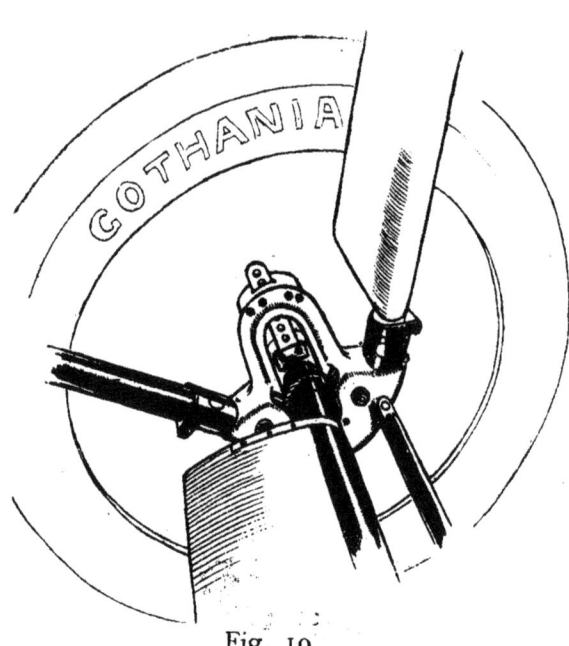

Fig. 10.

of the chord of the main planes, which point may be assumed to approach very closely the centre of gravity. This axle, as shown in the scale drawing at the end of the report, and also in the detail sketch reproduced herewith, moves up and down in guides against the action of two long compression springs concealed within the main undercarriage struts. A stout steel cable is passed over the axle and under two pulleys enclosed in the horn plate; thence it goes up inside the long springs to the heads of adjustable bolts, against which the upper ends of the springs abut. The axle is fitted with a large three-ply fairing attached by means of light straps, and at its outer end terminates in a tee piece, which slides up and down in a slot in the horn plate, and prevents the axle from turning round.

Only the front undercarriage strut is streamlined. It is stayed with a tube to the middle of the rear strut, and at this point the mudguard brackets are fitted.

The front pair of landing wheels, the fitting of which is to facilitate landing in the dark, are supported on an axle attached to the frame extension by bands of steel coil springs of the type usually found in the smaller German designs.

The front wheels are smaller in diameter and narrower in track than the main landing wheels.

In every case the forward extension of the undercarriage was very badly crumpled up, and it is noticeably light in construction compared with the massive main landing gear.

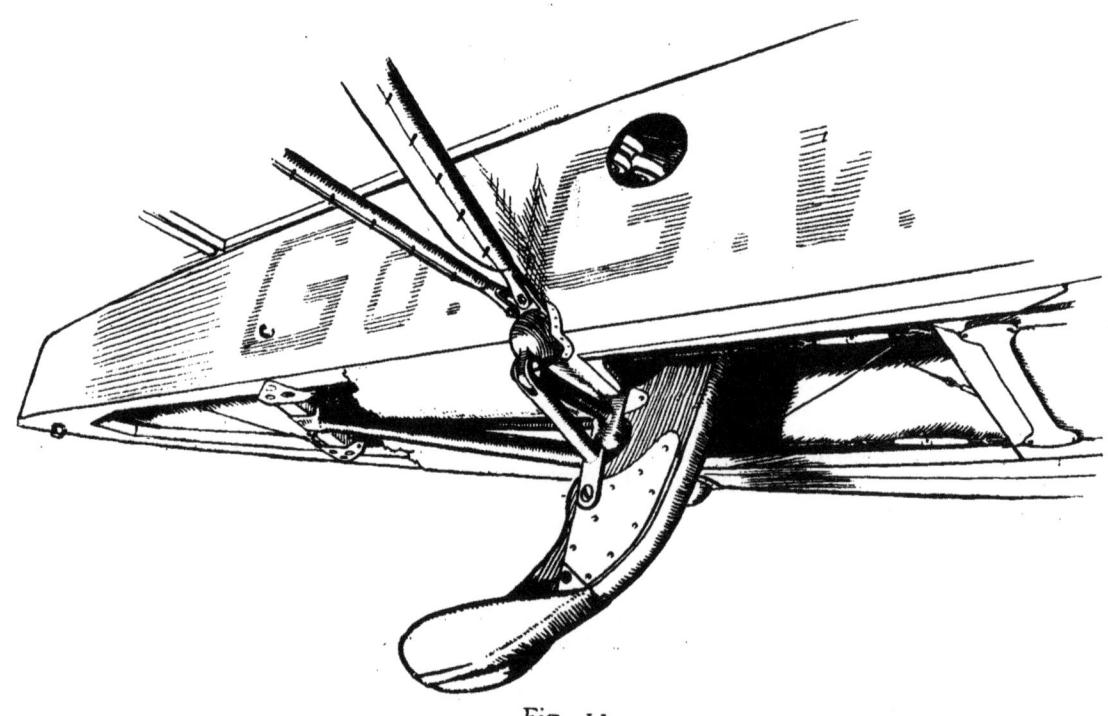

Fig. 11.

As might be expected, a very stout tail skid is fitted. This is shown in detail in Fig. 11.

The hinged skid is very strongly stayed in all directions. At its upper end it is attached with loops of steel coil springs to two tubular steel rings clipped to either side of the fuselage. A steel cable limits the distance through which the tail skid can move.

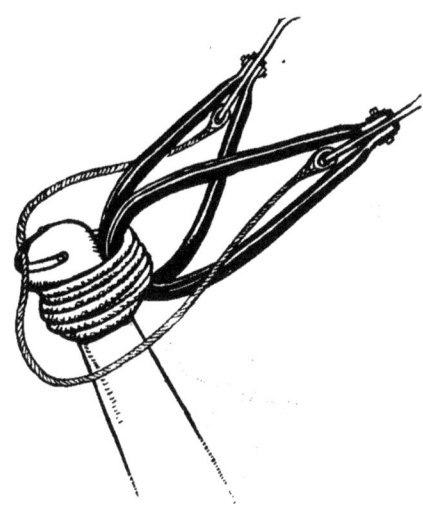

Fig. 12.

The body of the tail skid is of wood, but it is heavily reinforced with a steel shoe and with a steel front edge. Fig. 11 also shows the attachment of the lower tail struts to the bottom of the fuselage, and it will be seen that these are provided with sharp bars to discourage mechanics from lifting the tail by their means.

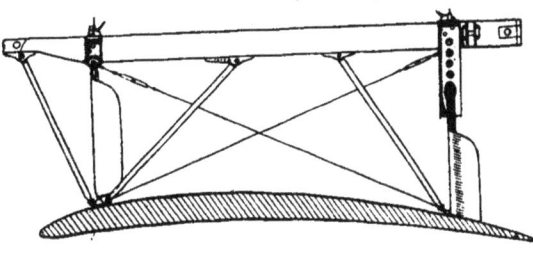

Fig. 13.

ENGINE MOUNTING.

The 260 H.P. 6-cylinder Mercedes engines are carried on bearers arranged as shown incidentally in the drawing of the undercarriage assembly, and illustrated with more detail in Fig. 13.

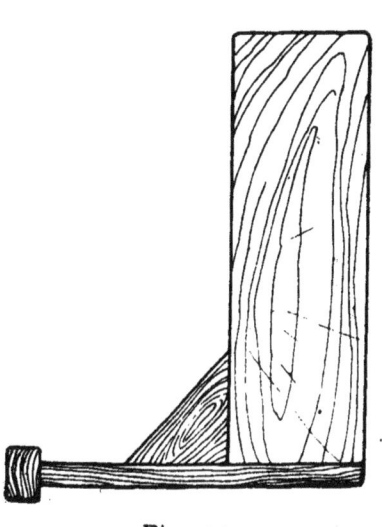

Fig. 14.

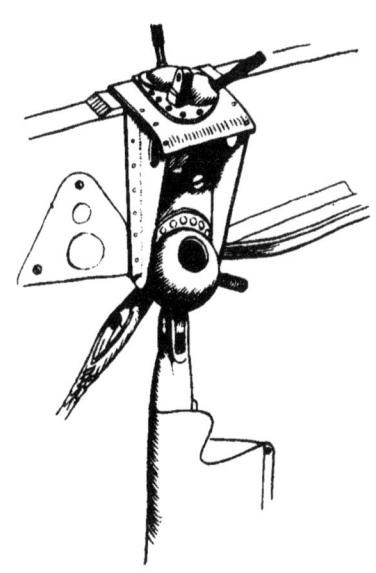

Fig. 15.

The bearers themselves are of wood, and between the main vertical supports on which they rest, are of the section shown in Fig. 14. They are attached to these main supports by ball joints of large diameter, and the struts are streamlined with casings of thin metal. These are shown in Fig. 15.

At their rear ends the engine bearers are united by a curved cross piece of hollow section, built up of sheet steel rivetted together. (Fig. 16.)

The engine bearers are triangulated to the plane section below them by cross wires as shown in Fig. 13, and also by diagonal steel tubes, the latter being attached by feet of the type shown in Fig. 17.

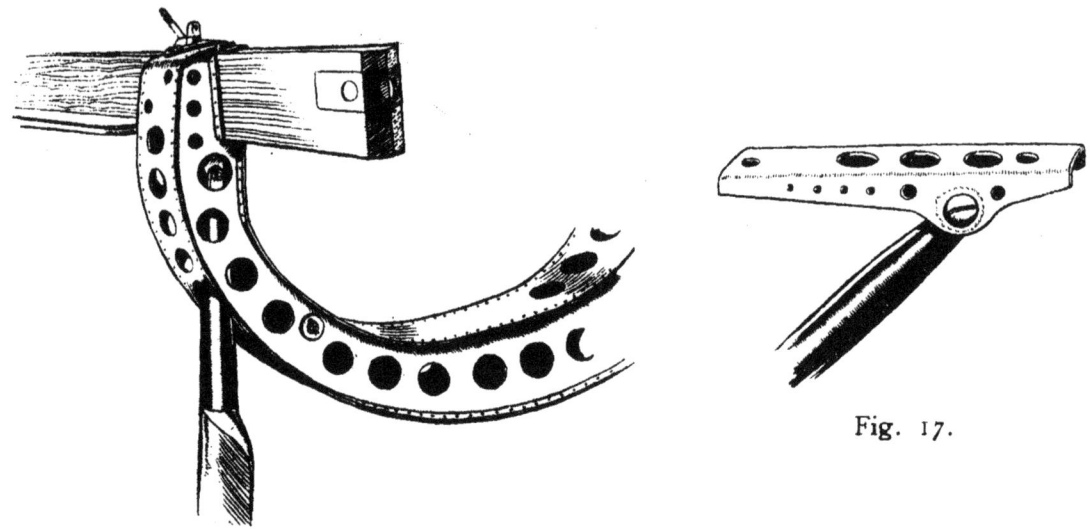

Fig. 16.   Fig. 17.

The bracket supporting the bearers in front entirely surrounds them, and at its upper end is provided with an attachment for the strut which unites the engine mounting to the top plane spar, and also with a ball and socket attachment for the undercarriage bracing cables.

At the bottom of the forward engine bearer support is attached one of the diagonal strengthening members of the forward undercarriage framework.

ENGINES.

In general the engines show no departures from the usual Mercedes practice, but there are a few points which are worthy of note.

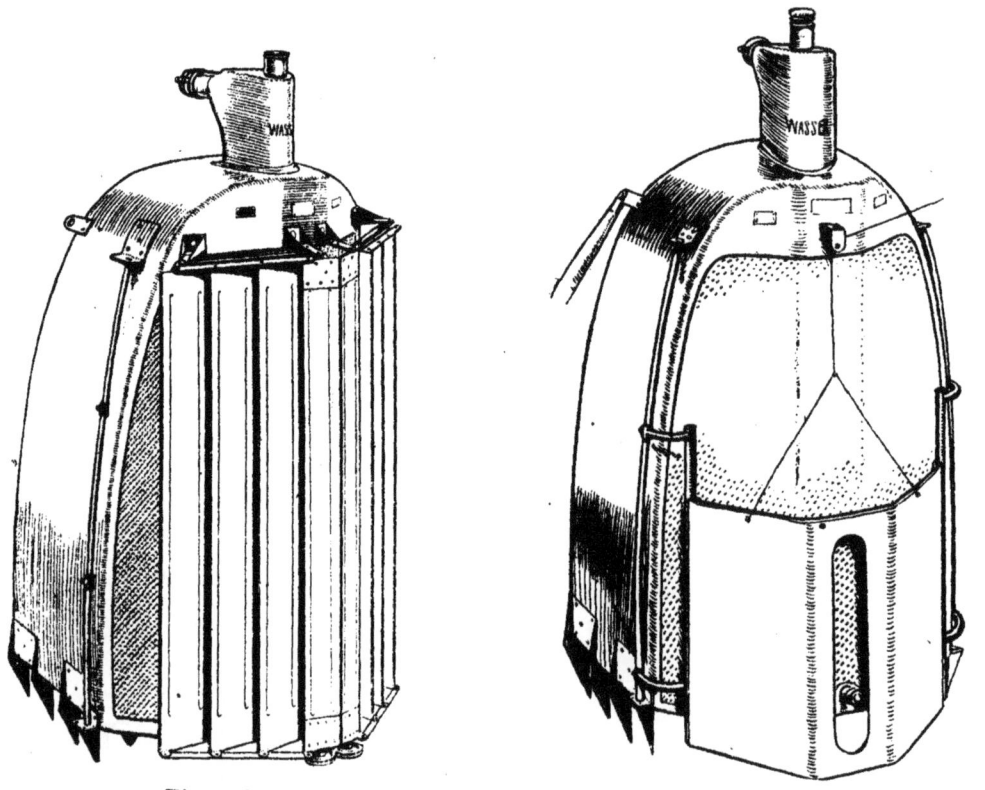

Fig. 18.   Fig. 19.

Two different kinds of radiators were employed on machines otherwise exactly similar, the principal difference between these radiators being the arrangement of the shutters; in one case a series of vertical panels is used, and in the other a simple sliding door is adapted to be raised or lowered so as to shield the radiator surface to the required degree.

Electrical thermometers of the usual pattern are fitted.

The radiator controls are placed one on each side of the pilot's cockpit, and are illustrated in Fig. 20.

Five different positions of the lever are provided for, and it works the shutters through return cables passing over a large aluminium pulley.

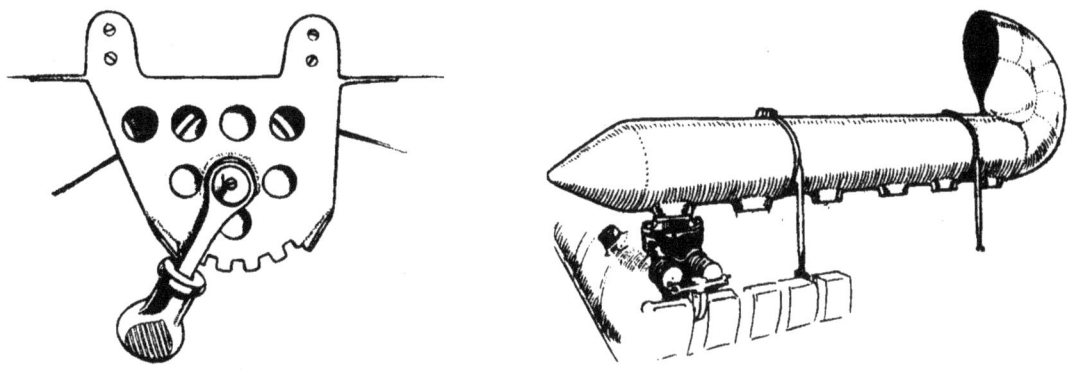

Fig. 20.   Fig. 21.

Two different kinds of silencer were found; the type illustrated in Fig. 21 is similar to that used on previous Gothas, and also on the Friedrichshafen machines. It consists of a sheet steel manifold of very light construction, containing no baffles or other means of restricting the outflow of gas.

The other type of exhaust box is shown in Fig. 22, and in this case it would appear that some attempt has been made not only to silence the exhaust, but also to prevent the aeroplane showing its whereabouts through the exhaust flames.

This new type of silencer has been reported upon as follows:—

The exhaust manifold has been altered in the spacing of the communications in order to fit a B.H.P. engine in a D.H. 9. The manifold consists of a cylinder 3 ft. 9 in. long and 6 in. in diameter; pointed nose and tail pieces are welded on, and fourteen cooling fins running lengthwise are fitted. Between the fins a number of ¼ in. diameter holes are drilled, forming a means of outlet for the exhaust gases, no baffle plates being fitted; the whole is made up of 20-gauge sheet steel, and is very flimsy in appearance.

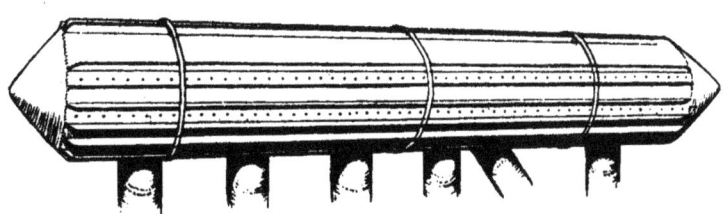

Fig. 22.

For testing this exhaust as a flame damper, a machine fitted with the manifold was flown at night with no navigation lights, and another machine was sent up to find it. As a silencer the manifold reduces the distance at which the machine is audible by a mean of about 4 per cent. No difficulty was experienced by the observing pilot in picking up the machine; although the flame usually seen at night was broken up, there was a stream of small sparks which made the aeroplane just as visible. In addition, it was noticed that the manifold became red hot when the machine was flown at full throttle.

CONTROLS.

All the Gotha machines brought down were fitted with the same type of control, though certain detail differences are noticed.

The ailerons are worked by a large diameter wheel by means of a chain and sprocket as shown in Fig. 23.

Limiting cables are fitted and attached to an adjustable clip on the column.

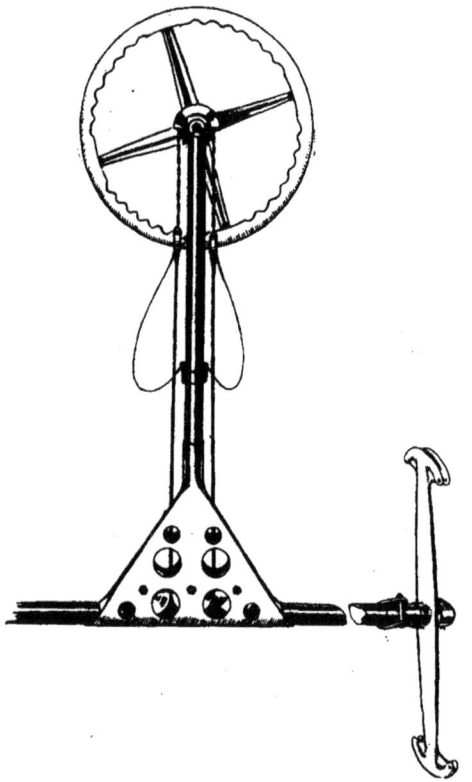
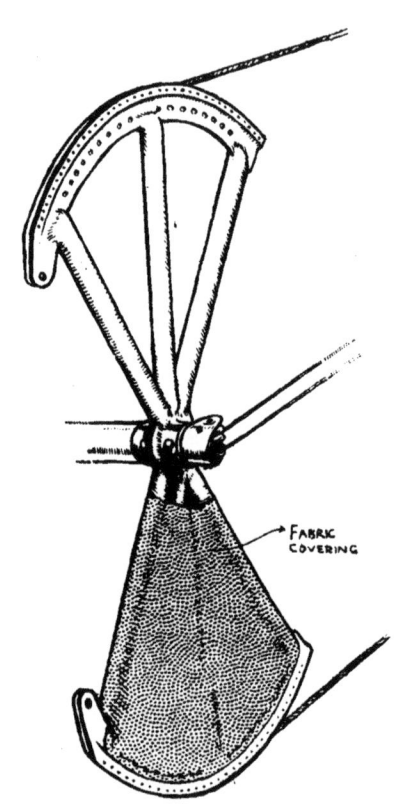

Fig. 23.   Fig. 24.

The wires are passed over pulleys and issue through the ends of the transverse rocking shaft, whence they pass through the planes between the leading edge and the leading spar of the lower wings.

At the extreme outer interplane strut they are taken over pulleys to the levers of the upper ailerons, which are connected to those of the lower ailerons by a light streamline strut. The horizontal rocking shaft extends through the side of the fuselage, and is there fitted in some cases with the simple form of double-ended crank shown in Fig. 23, but in others with the quadrant type of lever built up of steel tube, and illustrated in Fig. 24.

The elevator and rudder wires are led along the outside of the fuselage through guides.

The control wires for the elevator are duplicated, and in the case of the rudder a double crank is fitted on the rudder post. This is shown in Fig. 25.

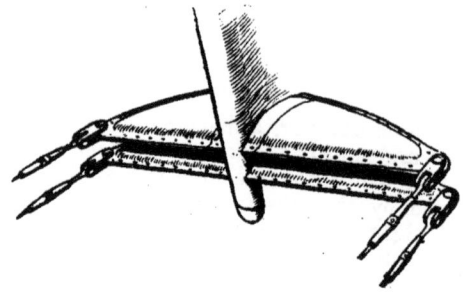

Fig. 25.

The rudder control bar is of the usual welded-up steel type, and is fitted with spring controlled heel rests. It is fitted with a grooved quadrant carrying the wires which pass over pulleys mounted in brackets on the inside of the fuselage walls. The rudder bar is shown incidentally in Fig. 27. No form of dual control is fitted. It is, however, of interest to note that whereas in the Friedrichshafen design means are provided both for adjusting the trim of the tail and for locking the controls in any desired position, the Gotha machine posesses neither of these refinements.

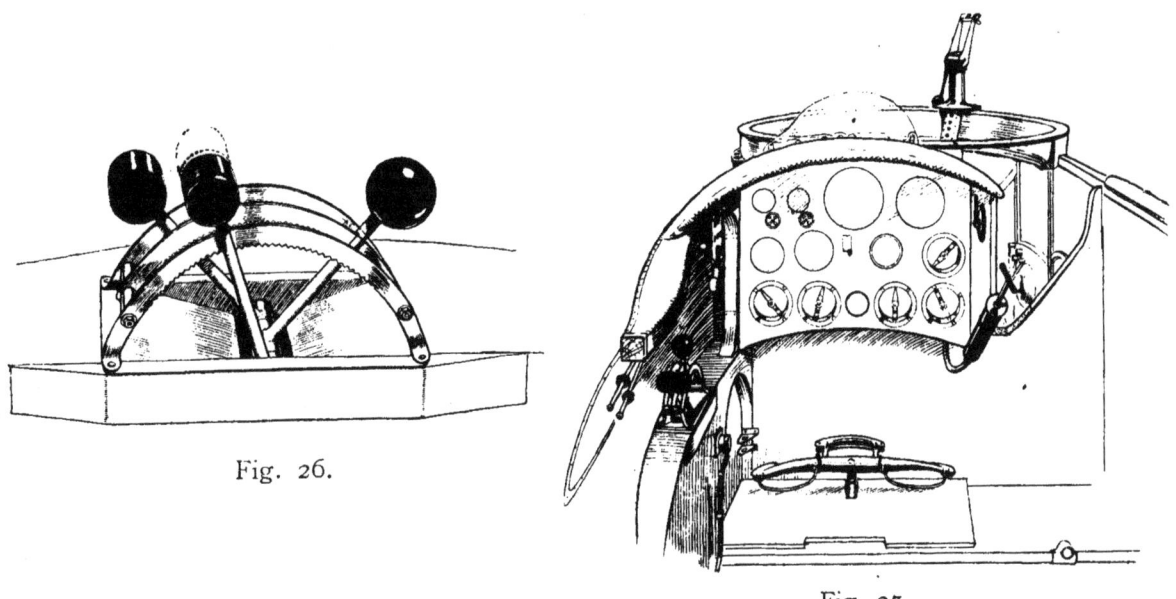

Fig. 26.

Fig. 27.

ENGINE CONTROLS.

The throttle levers are fitted on the left-hand side of the pilot's seat, which is also on the left-hand side of the fuselage. This control consists of two mallet-headed levers, which are shaped so as to be conveniently worked either together or separately; the cranks and rods which they operate are placed outside the main section of the fuselage, and are covered in with a streamline metal casing.

The engines are fitted, as is the usual Mercedes practice, with combination ignition and throttle controls; the function of the ball-headed third lever is not precisely known.

Fig. 28.

In front of the pilot is a dashboard arranged as shown in Fig. 27, containing the usual switches, gauges, instruments and control taps. One of the latter is shown in more detail in Fig. 28.

PETROL SYSTEM.

The two main petrol tanks carried in the forward portion of the fuselage are equal in size, and have a joint capacity of 175 gallons. They are made of sheet brass, and appear to be well provided with internal baffle plates.

On the left-hand upper wing, slightly to one side of the centre line of the machine, is a streamline gravity tank, strapped on to the upper surface, above which it projects; this gravity tank, which is used solely for starting purposes, has a capacity of about 10 gallons. It is filled from one or other of the main tanks by means of a hand-operated suction pump mounted on the right-hand side of the pilot's dash board, as shown in Fig. 27.

The two main tanks work under pressure; an air pump of the usual type is mounted within reach of the pilot.

ARMAMENT.

Two Parabellum guns are carried—one in the forward cockpit, and one in the rear. The former is carried on a large ring mounting, which is shown in Figs. 29 and 30. In order to allow access between this cockpit and that of the pilot, part of the ring is made to hinge out of the way like the flap of a counter. The ring is extensively perforated with

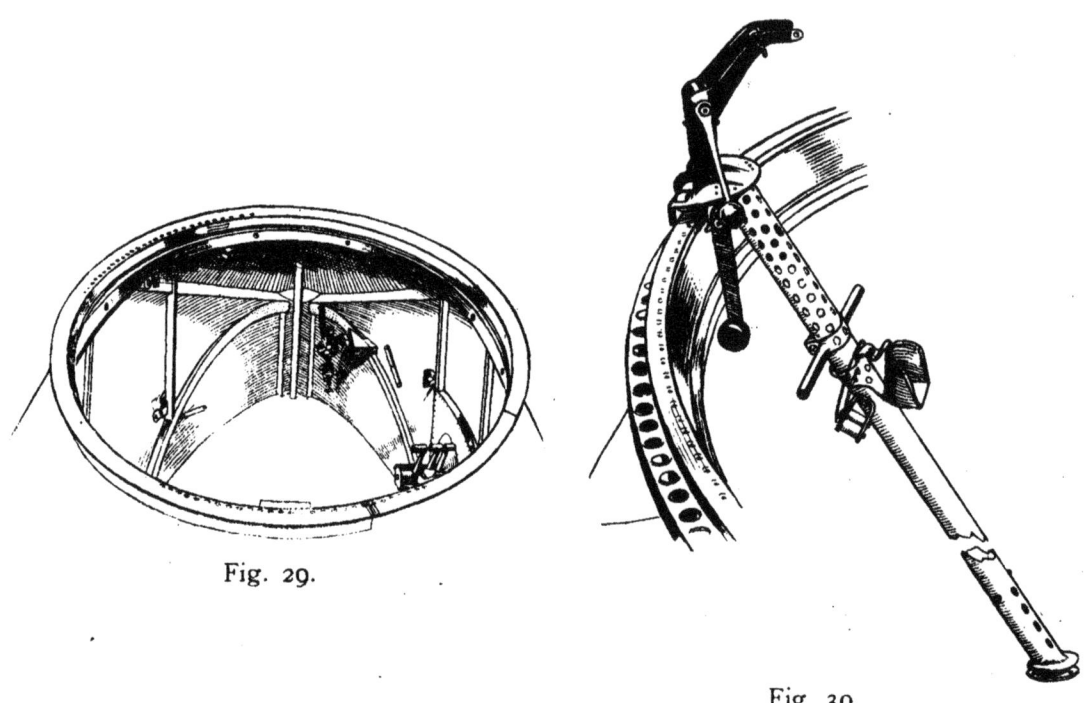

Fig. 29.

Fig. 30.

countersunk holes, apparently for lightening purposes. The holes of the hinged portion, together with the latch which secures them, are shown in Fig. 31. The gun is carried on a universally jointed bracket of the accepted design, which is furnished with an inclined extension, supported from the floor of the fuselage by a foot step bearing.

The gun carrier is fitted with two steel rollers, which rest on the ring mounting, outside of which is mounted a gallery of light metal fitted with numerous holes for the reception of Very pistol ammunition.

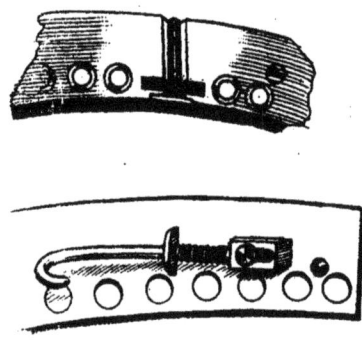

Fig. 31.

The rear gun is carried on a forked bracket, which slides over two rails made of bent steel tube, and mounted on the top surface of the fuselage as illustrated in Fig. 7. This gun carriage has a very limited arc of motion, and the usual expanded metal shields are fitted to prevent the gunner firing at the propeller, and possibly to prevent him leaning out far enough to be in danger of being struck by one of the blades.

On the floor of the after gunner's cockpit and close to the edge of the tunnel is a bracket designed for the reception of a second gun which would fire in a similar manner to that which was fitted on the earlier Gotha types. No guns fixed in this position have been found, and it is evident, therefore, that the upper gun is relied upon to answer all defensive requirements.

BOMBS.

The number and type of bombs carried on Gotha aeroplanes varies considerably, and the carriers are in consequence adapted to be easily removed and replaced by others of larger or smaller size, as the case may be.

The carriers used on the Gotha are exactly similar to those which have been found on A.E.G. and Friedrichshafen machines, and present no new features, with this exception, that on the Gotha each carrier is furnished with an electrical detector device which informs the

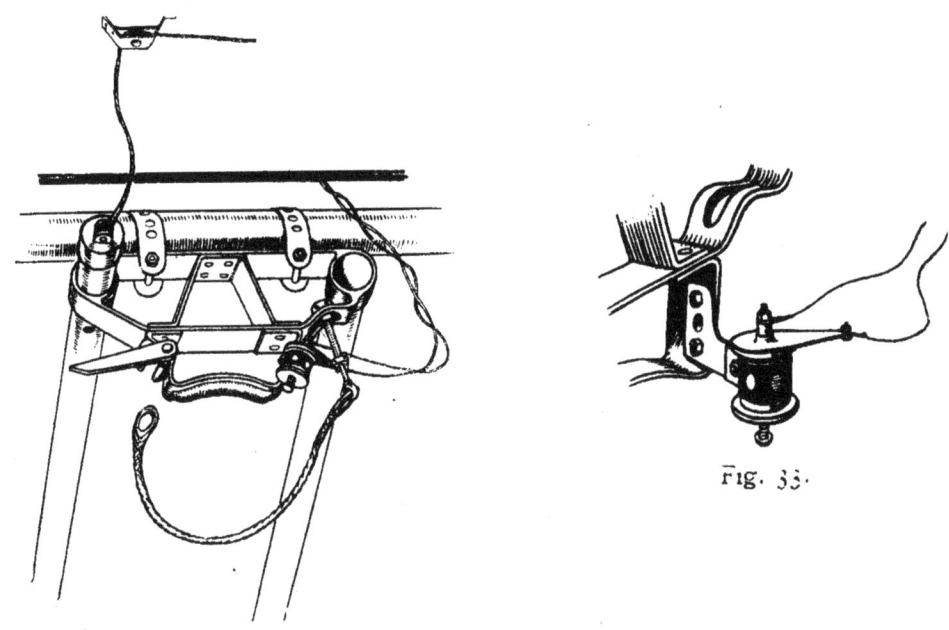

Fig. 32.

bomber that the projectile has actually left the carrier. This detector consists of a small switch, details of which are shown in Figs. 32 and 33, so that when the bomb leaves the carrier an electric lamp is illuminated inside the forward cockpit; this is carried out by means of a small spring-operated plunger switch.

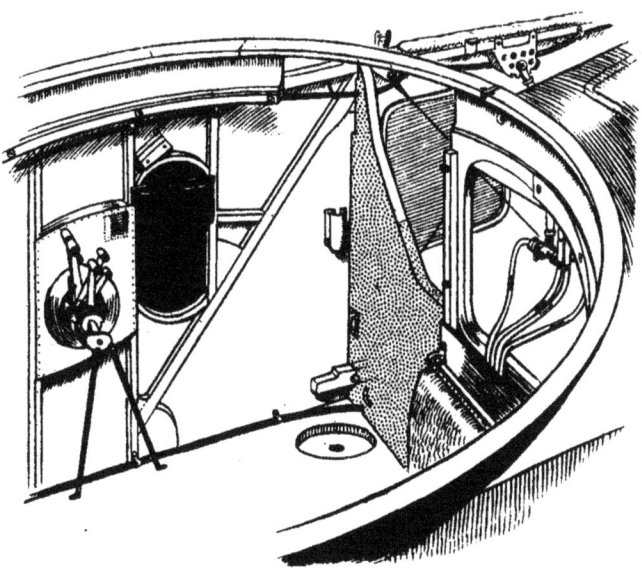

Fig. 34.

As a rule, eight bombs, each of 100 kg. weight, are carried—two being supported directly under the fuselage, and three on either side of the bottom plane centre section. Their release is effected by six small levers working the release gear through wires; each of these levers is painted a characteristic colour, and they are furthermore of different lengths, so that the bomber has no difficulty in pulling the right one. It would appear that each bomb carried on the centre section of the lower plane is released separately, and that probably the two bombs underneath the fuselage are discharged simultaneously. The levers are shown at the back of Fig. 34, which also illustrates the folding seat and the communication flap between the bomber's cockpit and that of the pilot. Both the forward cockpits are furnished with large celluloid windows, which have been blacked over in all cases so as to be opaque.

WIRELESS.

The machine is internally wired throughout for giving greater wireless capacity, and the dynamo for the system is driven direct by one of the engines. It also furnishes current for the heating of passengers' clothing, for which plugs are arranged at convenient points.

It will be noted in Fig. 34 that the floor in the corner of the cockpit is dished for the reception of the apparatus which carries the bobbin and the aerial wire.

INSTRUMENTS.

The usual array of engine revolution counters, thermometers, pressure gauges, etc., is fitted on the Gotha, but no new types were found.

FABRIC AND DOPE.

Both the fabric and dope on the Gotha aeroplanes conform to the usual German standard. The camouflage is similar to that of the Friedrichshafen, and consists of irregular polygons of various dark colours, which are printed on the fabric.

Gotha brought down by French A.A. Fire near Crochte, on 4-5 July, 1918.

The general construction of this machine appears to be similar to that described above in most respects, except for three modifications, which are worthy of note:—

1. A biplane tail unit. This is illustrated in the photographs, Figs. 48, 49, and 50. It is similar in design to that of the Handley-Page, and embodies two fins on either side of the fuselage between the planes of the tail. The rudders are hinged to the trailing edges of these fins. The measurements of the tail unit are as follows:—

Top elevator span	5 ft. 7 in.
Top elevator chord	2 ft. 7 in.
Bottom elevator span	5 ft. 3 in.
Bottom elevator chord	1 ft. 6¼ in.
Balance piece	11½ in. by 10¾ in.
Gap	2 ft. 9½ in.
Bottom tail planes each average fore and aft measurement	2 ft. 5 in.
Span along trailing edge, each	4 ft. 2 in.
Top tail plane, average fore and aft measurement	2 ft. 5 in.
Span along trailing edge	8 ft. 10 in.

This tail unit would appear to have been adapted in order to give the after gunner a better chance of attacking chasing aeroplanes, as the span is considerably smaller than that of the monoplane tail. It is constructed throughout of steel tubing.

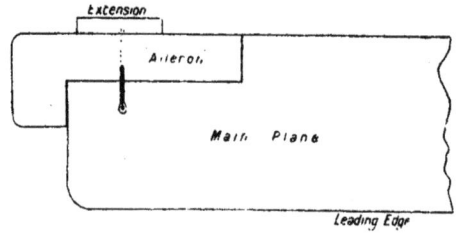

Fig. 35.

2. Extensions are fitted to the top ailerons as shown in the attached diagram (Fig. 35); it would appear from these that the lateral control of the Gotha has been found insufficient.

3. The undercarriages are arranged in a similar manner to those of the Friedrichshafen, that is to say, there is a two-wheeled undercarriage underneath each engine, and a third two-wheeled axle mounted on to the fore part of the fuselage: the wheels throughout are of equal size, carrying 810 by 125 mm. tyres.

Some details of the tail control are given in Figs. 36 and 37, from which it will be seen that double-ended levers with tubular tie rods are adopted for the rudders.

Fig. 36.   Fig. 37.

FOUR-ENGINED GIANT.

There are known to be a number of different types of giant bomb-carrying aeroplanes, distinguished by the four, five, or six engines with which they are fitted.

Examples of four-engined and five-engined aeroplanes have been brought down, but unfortunately, in all cases, in such a damaged condition that complete reconstruction is impossible.

The following particulars relate to a four-engined machine which landed near Betz on the night of June 1st. It was almost completely burnt by its occupants, and the metal parts alone remain, together with a few fragments of the body work.

The general arrangement of this aeroplane, together with the principal dimensions, is given in the accompanying drawings (Figs. 39, 40, and 41).

In contra-distinction to the two-engined machine, there is considerably more steel in the construction, and this material is used in place of wood for the rear portion of the fuselage.

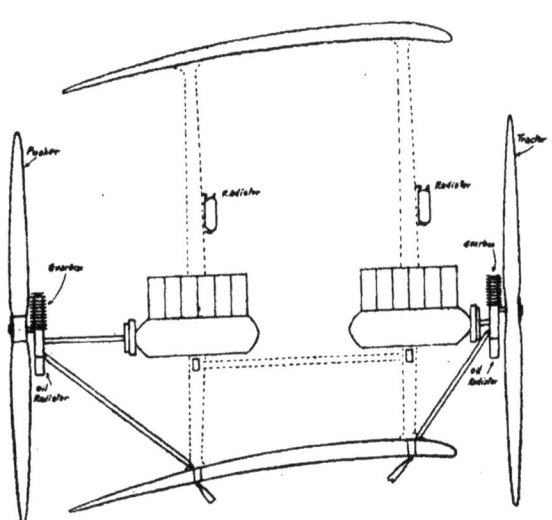

Fig. 38.

The principal point of interest is the mounting of the four engines, all of which are of the 260 H.P. Maybach type, six cylinders in a line; the horse-power has been forced up to 300, giving 1,200 H.P. in all. They are placed end to end, as shown in Fig. 38, and each drives a separate screw.

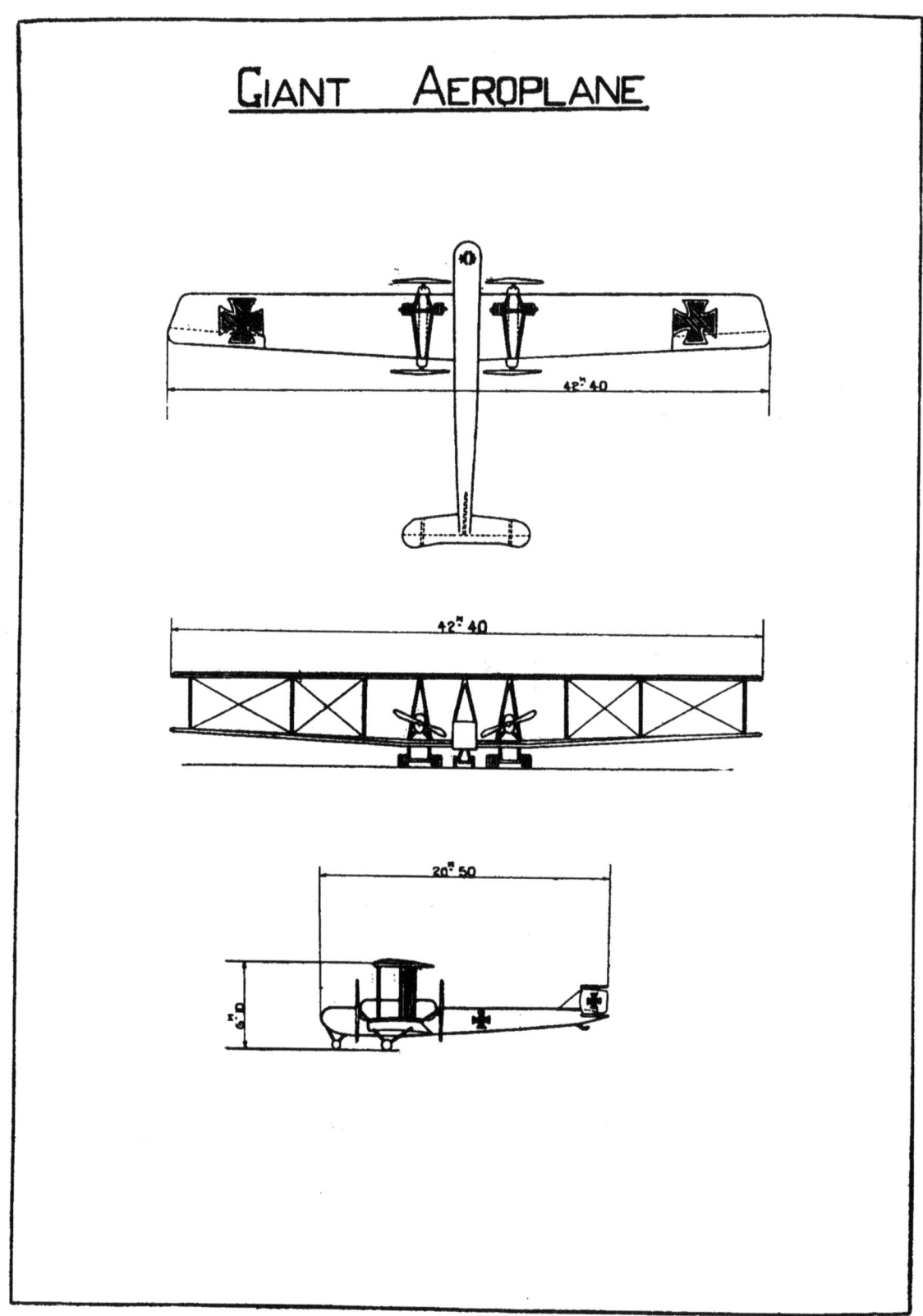

Fig. 39.

In order to bring the centre of gravity of the machine sufficiently far forward, the weight of the two engines is massed towards the leading edge of the main plane; by driving the screws through shafts and reduction gears, the necessity of cutting away large sections from the planes to give room for the rear propellers has been avoided.

The arrangement of the engine unit on each side of the fuselage is diagrammatically shown in Fig. 38, from which it will be seen that the two engines are placed close together, and that the rear motor is some little distance away from its screw. The forward engine is, however, mounted close up to the tractor screw.

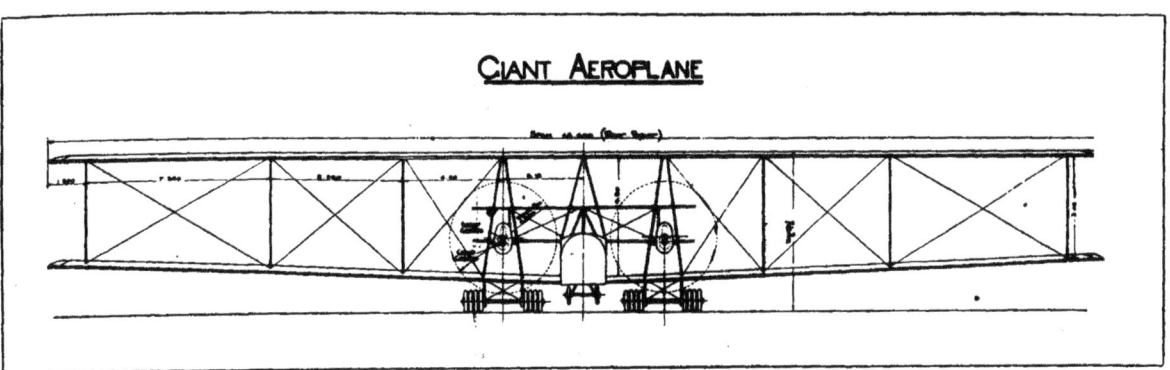

Fig. 40.

The employment of shafts and reduction gears necessitates fly wheels on the engines. These are .4 metre in diameter, and made of cast iron. The tubular driving shafts between the fly wheel and the gear box are furnished with flexible leather couplings. These are of a novel type, and consist of a male and female drum, each furnished with circumferential notches, between which are interposed a series of flat leather strips. The female drum forms part of the fly wheel.

The gear box consists of a casing of aluminium, provided with cooling fins, which may be seen in Figs. 52 and 54.

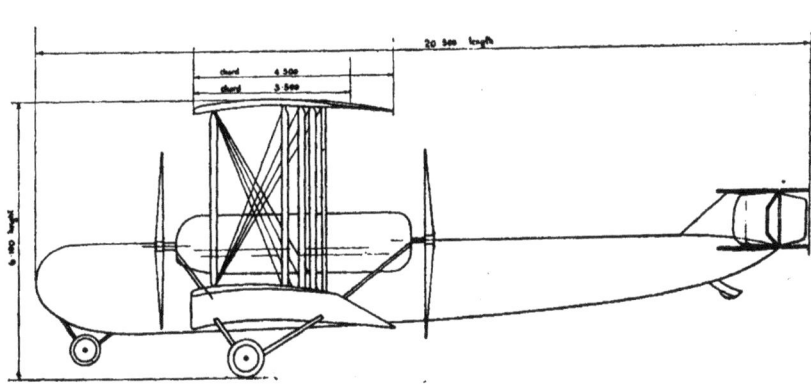

Fig. 41.

Beneath each gear case is a small radiator for cooling the lubricating oil circulated through the engine. This radiator can be seen in Fig. 52, and consists apparently of a flat semi-circular tank, fitted with numerous transverse tubes of fairly large diameter (about 20 mm.) in a manner similar to that of a honeycomb radiator. A pump mounted at the base of the radiator is also furnished with an electrical thermometer, giving a reading on a dial in the cockpit.

Each engine is fitted with a self-starting arrangement of the type usually fitted to Maybach motors. The exhaust pipe may be closed by means of a shutter, and all the cylinders can be filled with gas from the carburettor by means of a large hand-pump, for which purpose all the valves are held open. When these valves are closed, and the starting magneto operated, the engine fires and continues running. Each engine has its own radiator, which is mounted directly above it, and supported by struts and stay wires at a point about half-way between the top and bottom planes. These radiators are of the type usually fitted to D.F.W. machines. They are rectangular in shape, with their greater length placed horizontally, and the radiating surface consists of a series of zig-zag tubes placed vertically.

The engine bearers consist of stout ash spars, reinforced with multi-ply wood. Owing to the burnt condition of the machine no information could be obtained as to the engine controls, and the screws were also too badly damaged to yield definite information as to dimension and construction, though they appear to be made chiefly of ash and covered with a thin veneer.

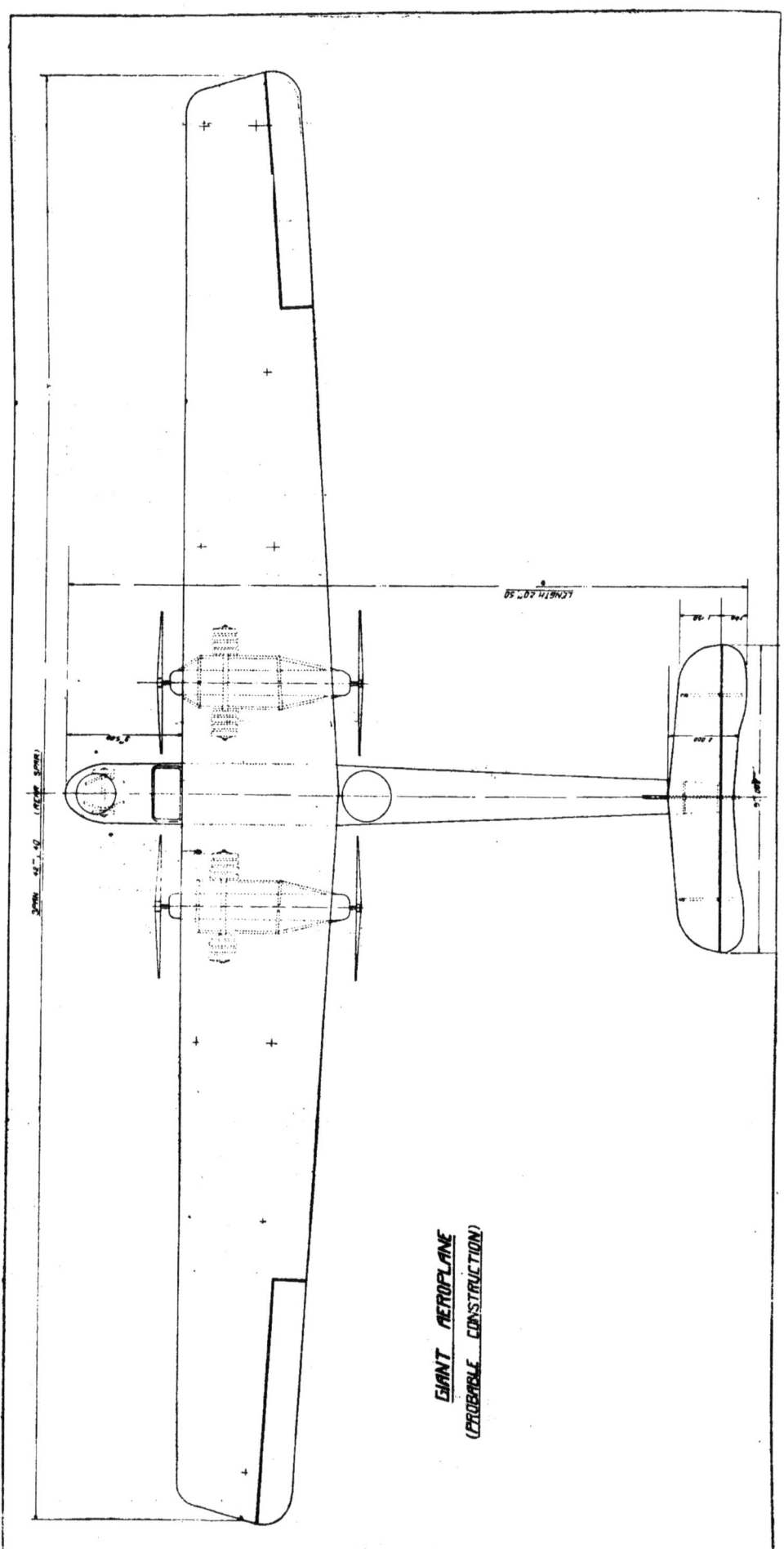

Fig. 42.

WING CONSTRUCTION.

The spars are shown in Fig. 43, built up very elaborately in sections, and consisting of no less than seven sections of spruce, reinforced with multi-ply on each side, and finally carefully bound with doped fabric.

The spars of the lower wings are continuous, that is to say, they run right across the centre section of the fuselage, to the longerons of which they are secured, contrary to the usual practice, in which special compression members, forming part of the fuselage construction, are employed. The wing surface, both upper and lower, is divided into three sections, of which the middle section extends to the engine mountings on each side. The spars in this section are both at right angles to the axis of the fuselage. At each side of the middle section

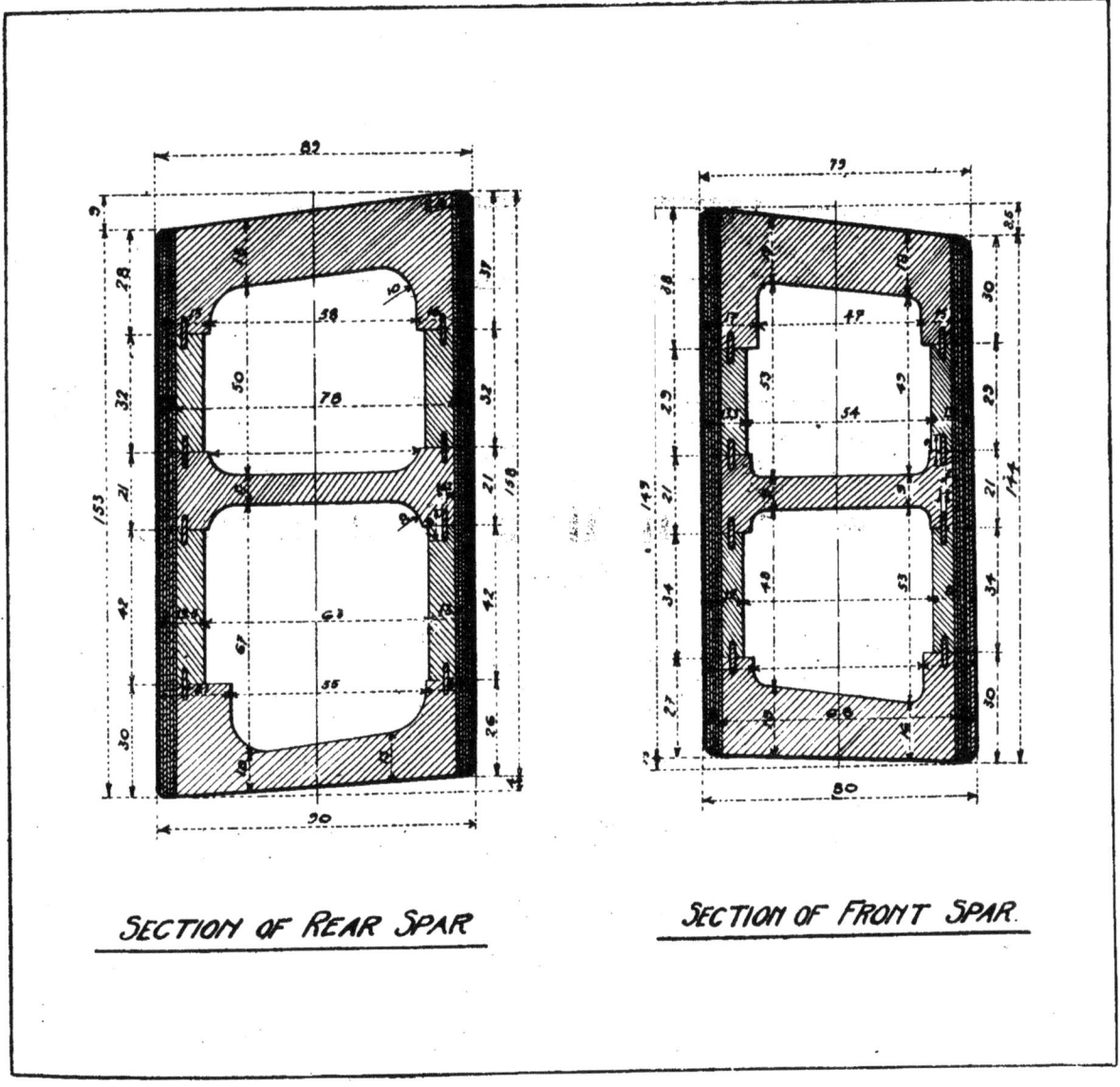

Fig. 43.

the leading edge of the wings is boldly swept back as well as tapered. The rear spars of the wings, together with those of the centre section, form a straight line from wing-tip to wing-tip, but the front spars are swept back.

The ribs, of which a detail drawing is given in Fig. 44, are built up, and of girder form.

Between the leading edge and the leading spar, numerous extra ribs occur in addition to the main ribs. Internal bracing against drag takes the form of steel tubular compression members and steel cables, the former being placed at a point coincident with the attachment of each interplane strut. An additional bracing is installed, of which the compression member consists of a double rib placed half-way between the struts. In each case the bracing wires pass obliquely right through the spars.

The ribs are mounted parallel to the line of flight.

The disposal of the spars is as follows:—

Top Plane.—

Leading edge to centre of leading spar	1 ft. 9½ in.
Distance between centres of spars	5 ft. 7½ in.
Trailing edge to centre of rear main spar	5 ft.

Bottom Plane.—

Leading edge to centre of leading spar	1 ft. 7½ in.
Distances between centres of main spars	5 ft. 1 in.
Trailing edge to centre of rear main spar	5 ft. (approximately).

The trailing edge of this aeroplane was too badly damaged to permit of this measurement being given accurately.

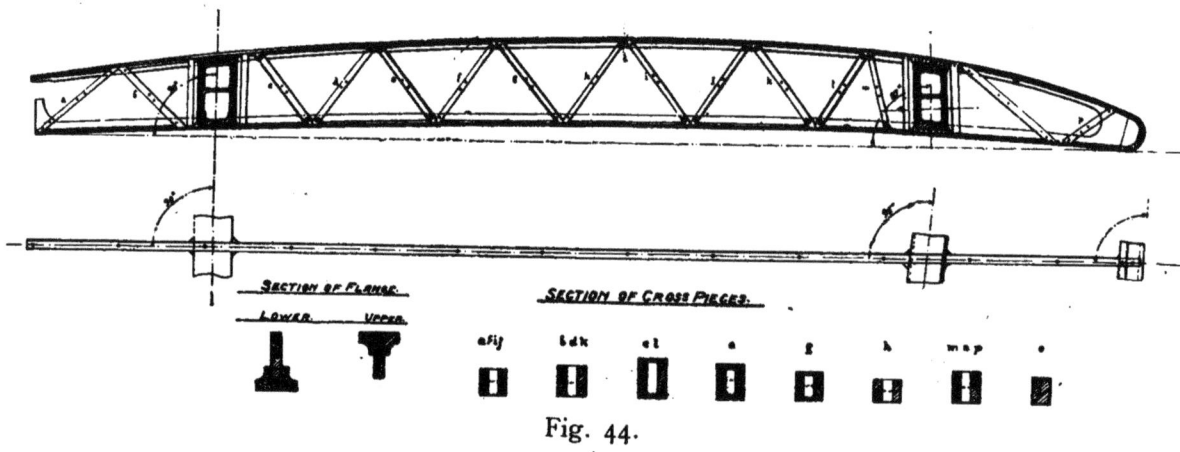

Fig. 44.

Between the interplane struts the rear spars are thinned down in width, but their depth remains practically constant from root to tip. Such tapering as exists is so arranged as to promote a decided wash-out of the angle of incidence near the tip. This is done by tapering the front spar on its upper edge, and the rear spar on its lower edge.

AILERONS.

These are on the top planes only, and are provided with a framework of steel tubing. They are not balanced, and the controls are led in the usual manner through the bottom plane from the aileron lever.

The span of each aileron is 22 ft. 5 in., and the chord 3 ft. 4 in.

INTER-PLANE STRUTS.

These are of large-diameter steel tube, covered in with a streamline fairing consisting of three-ply mounted on a light rib-work of wood.

BRACING.

The attachment of the bracing cables to the spars is somewhat similar to the bracing of the Fokker fuselage; that is to say, the wires, instead of being anchored at each end to an eyebolt, are double, and are looped round the spar, to which is fixed a grooved channel-piece for the reception of the cable. It is difficult to see that any advantage is gained by this arrangement.

TAIL UNIT.

A biplane tail, somewhat similar to that of the Handley-Page, is fitted. The fixed tail planes, the angle of incidence of which can be adjusted through small limits, are of wooden construction, and have the following dimensions:—

Span each side of fuselage	12 ft. 4 in.
Chord (average)	4 ft. 10 in.
Gap	6 ft. 9½ in.

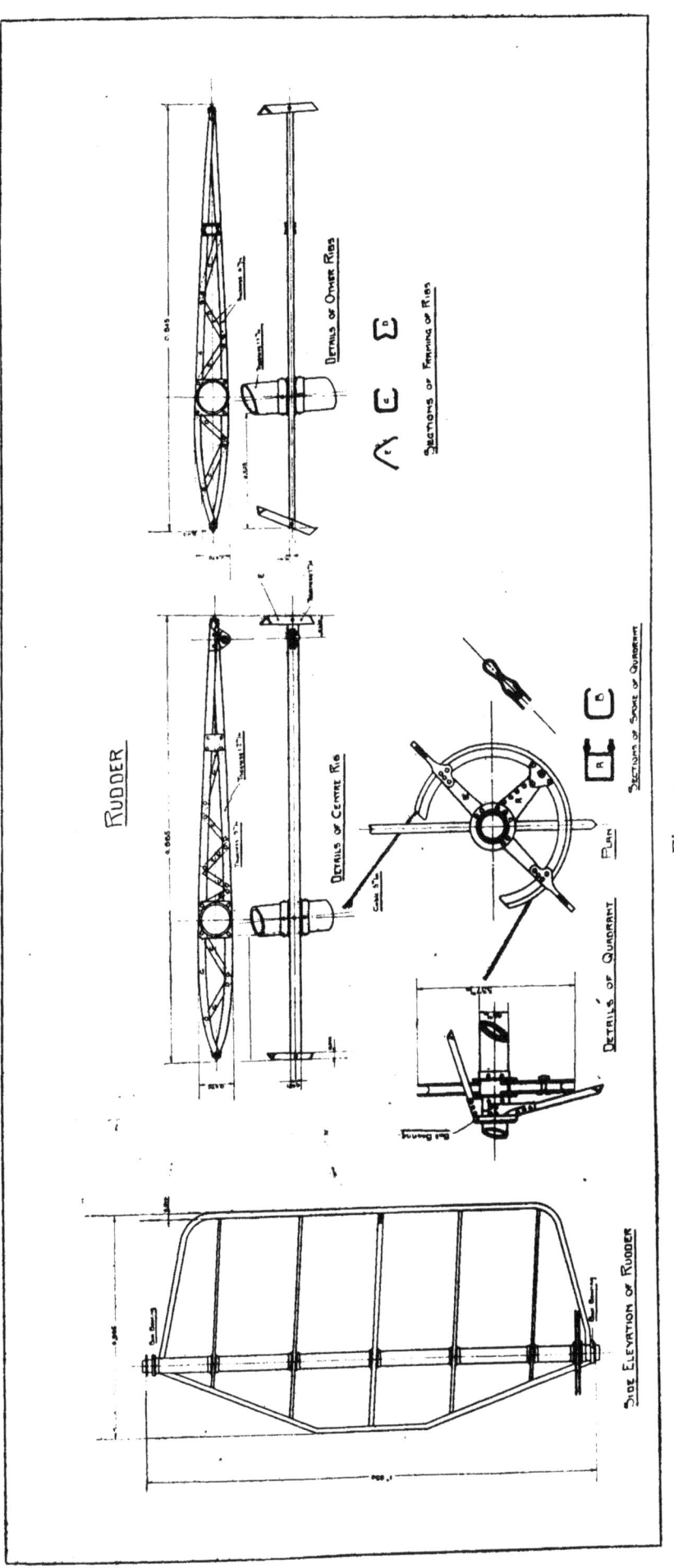

Fig. 45.

ELEVATORS.

These are fitted to both the top and bottom tail planes, and are of aluminium construction, the ribs, being of girder form, somewhat similar in construction to the ribs of the main planes. The elevators are not balanced; the top and bottom elevators are fitted with independent control levers, but are presumably operated together from the control stick. Their dimensions are as follows:—

Span	28 ft 6 in.
Chord at tip	2 ft. 4 in.
Chord at centre	1 ft. 6 in.

FINS.

There are three fins; two outer ones forming interplane struts, and an inner central one of triangular shape.

RUDDERS.

The framework of these organs is built up of aluminium in the manner set forth in detail in Fig. 45. This also shows the quadrant at the foot of the rudder posts by means of which they are operated; each rudder post is fitted with ball bearings, both top and bottom.

UNDERCARRIAGE.

Beneath each engine section is an undercarriage consisting of a massive axle fitted with four wheels at each end. This axle is attached by india-rubber shock absorbers to the tubular steel V-struts which form extensions of the engine bearer struts. A third undercarriage is mounted under the forward part of the fuselage, and consists of an axle with one pair of wheels.

ARMAMENT.

Only two gun mountings were found in the wreckage; they were fitted to a revolving turret in the gunner's cockpit. The mountings are of the fork type, and are situated on opposite sides of the circle. No arrangements for firing under the tail were found, nor was there evidence of a forward gun mounting.

BOMB GEAR.

Two steel tubular frameworks are fitted, one on either side of the fuselage. They are apparently adapted to carry very large bombs, probably of 1,000 kg. each; the release gear appears to be similar to that used on the Friedrichshafen, and already reported upon.

FIVE-ENGINED GIANT.

A 5-engined bomber was brought down near Talmas on the 10th of August, but unfortunately, owing to the explosion of one of its bombs, the machine was damaged beyond hope of reconstruction.

Some of its components have been recovered, and of these, photographs are given in Figs. 66 to 81.

The principal item of interest is the gear box, which is used for all five engines, each of which is a 300-H.P. Maybach of the standard 6-cylinder vertical type.

The power plants are arranged as follows:—In the nose of the machine is one engine driving a tractor screw. On each side of the fuselage, supported by the wings, is a long pair of engine bearers carrying two engines apiece, which drive tractor and pusher screws in a manner exactly similar to that set forth in Fig. 38.

The use of the gear box and driving shafts necessitates the employment of a fly wheel on the engine, to which is added the female portion of a flexible coupling of the type already described.

Whereas the gear box in the 4-engined Giant, of which notes have already been given in this report, is of a somewhat crude type employing external driving shafts between the gear box and the engine, in the 5-engined machine the gear-box design is considerably improved. The casing consists, as shown in Photograph No. 66, of a massive aluminium casting provided with four feet which are bolted to the engine bearers.

Two kinds of gear boxes are employed. These differ only in over-all dimensions and the length of the propeller shaft.

The larger type is used for the pusher screw in order to obviate the necessity of cutting a slice out of the trailing edge of the main planes.

All the gear boxes were very badly damaged except that which is shown in Fig. 66. This is the longer type, but it would appear that the shorter design is very similar in appearance.

In each case the gear reduction is 21—41.

Plain spur pinions are used having a pitch of 22 mm. and a width across the teeth of 75 mm. The diameter of the smaller of the driving pinions is 162.5 mm., and that of the larger pinion 282 mm.

The larger pinion is as shown in Fig. 72, considerably dished, but the web is not lightened by any perforations.

The over-all dimensions of the gear box as represented in Fig. 66, is as follows:—

Length, 1,025 mm.
Breadth, 675 mm.
Height, 535 mm.

The driving pinion runs on two large diameter roller bearings carried in gunmetal housings supported in the inner end of the gear box. This part is split vertically, and united by the usual transverse bolts, whilst the conical-shaped portion of the box is solid. The usual oil-thrower rings of helical type are fitted.

At its outer end the pinion shaft terminates in a ring of serrations which engage with serrations provided in the male portion of the flexible coupling, these two parts being held together with bolts and clamping plates. The engine is thus close up against the gear box, in contradistinction to the design of the 4-engine power plant. There is practically no external shaft at all. The larger pinion is mounted on a hollow shaft of 92 mm. diameter, carried on roller bearings at each end for radial load, and furnished at the nose end with ball thrust bearings.

In the short type of gear box the larger pinion shaft is left solid, and it would appear that the gear box casing, instead of being made in three pieces, is made in two pieces, i.e., the whole box is simply split vertically.

Reference to Photograph No. 67 will show that the smaller pinion shaft projects right through the gear box, and at its outer end carries a projection fitted with a small ball thrust race. This projection acts as a drive for the oil pump, which is mounted on the oil radiator used in connection with each gear box.

It is worthy of notice that the German designers have now fully realised the importance of using geared engines for weight carrrying aeroplanes, and are apparently satisfied with the external gear-box principle, although in this case they have made it a very ponderous affair indeed. Needless to say, a great amount of the weight could have been saved if 12-cylinder engines had been used instead of 6-cylinder.

The weights of the gear box and its attachments are as follows:—

Gear box, long type, 280 lbs.
Fly wheel and female clutch, 44 lbs.
Male clutch, 5 lbs.
Oil radiator, 12½ lbs.

This it will be seen represents an additional weight of considerably more than 1 lb. per h.p.

The oil radiator used in conjunction with each gear box is of a roughly semi-circular shape, and is slung underneath the main transverse members of the engine bearers so that it comes immediately beneath the large feet of the gear box, as shown in Fig. 68. This radiator is entirely of steel construction, and embraces sixty-five tubes of approximately 20 mm. internal diameter. These are expanded and sweated into the end plates, to one of which is fitted a stout flange, against which is bolted a small gear pump which constantly circulates the oil from the gear box case through the radiator.

This gear pump is driven by a flexible shaft from the small pinion, the shaft and its casing being in all respects similar to those employed for engine revolution counters. As shown in the Photograph Fig. 67, which illustrates the complete gear box upside down, this flexible drive is taken off a small worm gear.

It will also be seen that underneath the oil sump of the gear box proper an electrical thermometer is fitted, which communicates with a dial on the dashboard.

It is a little difficult to see what object can be served by this thermometer, unless it be to indicate the desirability of throttling down a little in the event of the oil getting unduly hot, as there is no apparent means of controlling the draught of air through the oil radiator.

Fitted on each gear box and working in connection with the oil circulation is a filter of the type shown in Fig. 74. This is provided with an aluminium case and a detachable gauze cylinder through which the oil passes.

The arrangement of the gear box is such that the axis of the propeller is raised about 220 mm. above that of the engine crankshaft.

The construction of the long engine bearers is not without interest, as amongst other things, it indicates that German manufacturers are finding themselves short of suitable timber. Each bearer, as shown in Fig. 46, consists of a spruce or pine central portion, to which are applied, top and bottom, five laminations of ash. On each side are glued panels of 3-ply, about ⅛ in. thick.

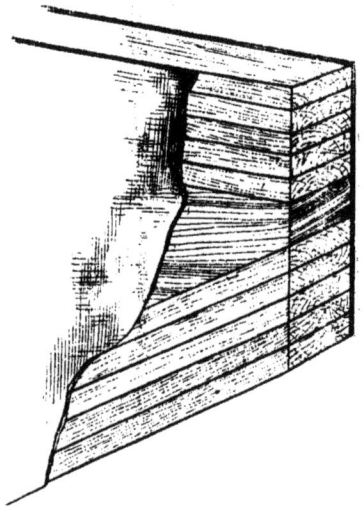

Fig. 46.

The engine bearers taper sharply at each end, and are strengthened by massive steel girders under each gear box. One of these girders, which is a single-piece welded construction, is illustrated in the Photograph, Fig. 76.

The screws revolve at approximately half the speed of the engine, and having therefore a moderately light centrifugal load to carry, are made of a common wood that would scarcely be safe for direct driving screws.

Although fitted to 300-H.P. Maybach engines, they are marked 260 p.s. (h.p.) Mercedes. The diameter is 4.30 meters, and the pitch 3.30, for the pusher screw, but unfortunately, owing to the propellers being badly damaged, not only by the crash, but by fire, it is not possible to state whether the tractor screws are of the same dimensions and pitch.

The construction is very interesting; each screw is made of seventeen laminations of what appears to be soft pine, and these laminations are themselves in pieces, and do not run continuously from tip to tip. They are, of course, staggered, so that the joints in successive layers do not coincide. Two plies of very thin birch veneer are wrapped round the blades. The grain of this veneer runs across the blade instead of along it.

It is difficult to say from the appearance of the screw whether this veneer has been put on in the form of 2-ply or as two separate layers, one after the other.

Among other details salved from the wreckage is the engine control. This is illustrated in Photograph No. 75, and is a very massive affair. It consists of five stout steel tubular levers, two of which it will be noticed have become unbrazed in the fire which broke out when the machine crashed.

The levers are fitted with ratchets so that each one can be operated individually, but the presence of the large-diameter toothed wheel in the centre of the lever shaft would seem to indicate that all five levers could, when desired, be controlled simultaneously. This fitting had, however, been very badly fused, and it is impossible to give details with certainty.

A smaller fitting recovered from the wreckage is illustrated in Photograph No. 70, and consists of a windmill of a type similar to that used on the D.H. 9 aeroplane. It is mounted at the top of an aluminium tube, but it is not possible to say for what purpose this mill is employed.

A small and very heavy rotary pump, found in the wreckage, is shown in Photograph No. 70. This is possibly the hand driven petrol pump, though it would appear unusually massive for this purpose.

The Douglas type of engine, carried for the purpose of driving the dynamo of the wireless and heating installation, is illustrated in Photographs No. 77, 79, 80, and 81, which show various views of the motor and generator. The engine is a very close copy of the $2\frac{3}{4}$ H.P. Douglas, and is made by Bosch. The fly wheel, as shown in Photograph No. 70, is furnished with radial vanes which induce a draught through a sheet-iron casing, and direct it past cowls on to the cylinder heads and valve chests.

The generator is direct-driven through the medium of a pack of flat leaf springs, which act as dogs, and engage with the slots on the fly-wheel boss, as shown in Fig. 81.

What appears to be a transformer, used in conjunction with the wireless set, is illustrated in Photograph No. 78.

The ponderous tail skid of this machine is illustrated in Fig. 47. It is built up of laminations of ash, and furnished with a heavy steel shoe and a large universal attachment.

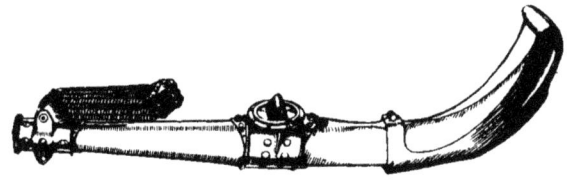

Fig. 47.

SPECIAL NOTE.

A complete and detailed report on the above-mentioned gear box, giving the fullest possible information and analysis of metals, etc., will shortly be published.

W. G. A.

Ap.D(L).

J. G. WEIR,

Brigadier-General,

Controller, Technical Department.

Three views of the biplane tail and fuselage of the two-engined Gotha.

Fig. 48.

Fig. 49.

Fig. 51.
Four-engined Giant. Maybach Flywheel and Female Clutch.

Fig. 52.
Four-engined Giant. Gear Box and Oil Radiator.

Fig. 53.
Four-engined Giant. Radiator.

Fig. 54.

Four-engined Giant. Gear Box and External Driving Shaft of Pusher Screw.

Fig. 55.

Four-engined Giant. Empennage.

Fig. 56.
Four-engined Giant. Empennage.

Fig. 57.
Four-engined Giant. Undercarriage.

Fig. 59.
Four-engined Giant. General View of Wreckage.

Fig. 60.
Four-engined Giant. Rear end of Fuselage and Tail Skid

Fig. 61.
Four-engined Giant. Power Plant.

Fig. 62.
Four-engined Giant. Main Planes and Ailerons.

Fig. 63.
Four-engined Giant. Attachment of Struts and Compression Tube.

Fig. 65.
Four-engined Giant.   General View of Wreckage.

Fig. 66.
Five-engined Giant.   Long Gear Box, complete with Male Clutch.

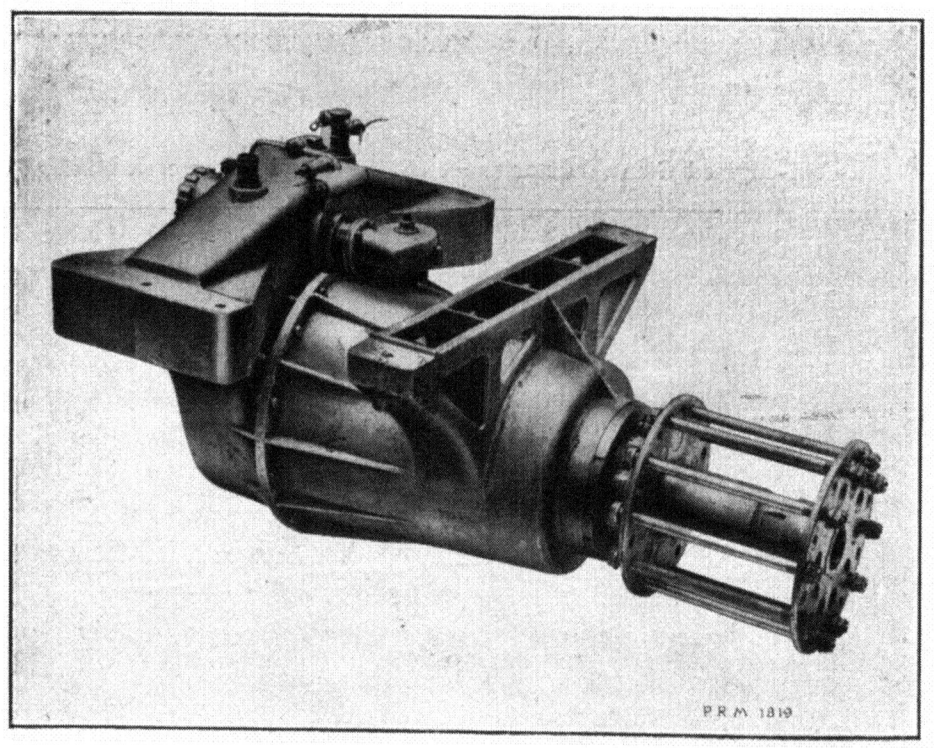

Fig. 67.
Five-engined Giant.   Long Gear Box seen from underside.

Fig. 68.
Five-engined Giant. Broken Gear Box (long type), with Bearers and Oil Radiator.

Fig. 69.
Five-engined Giant. Driving Pinion.

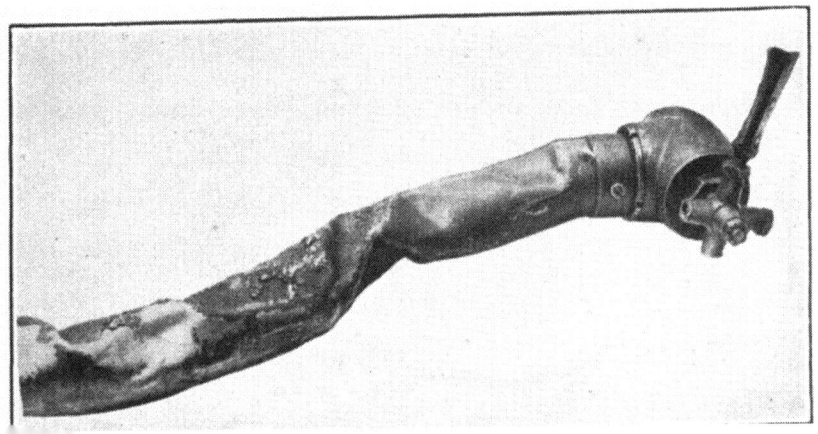

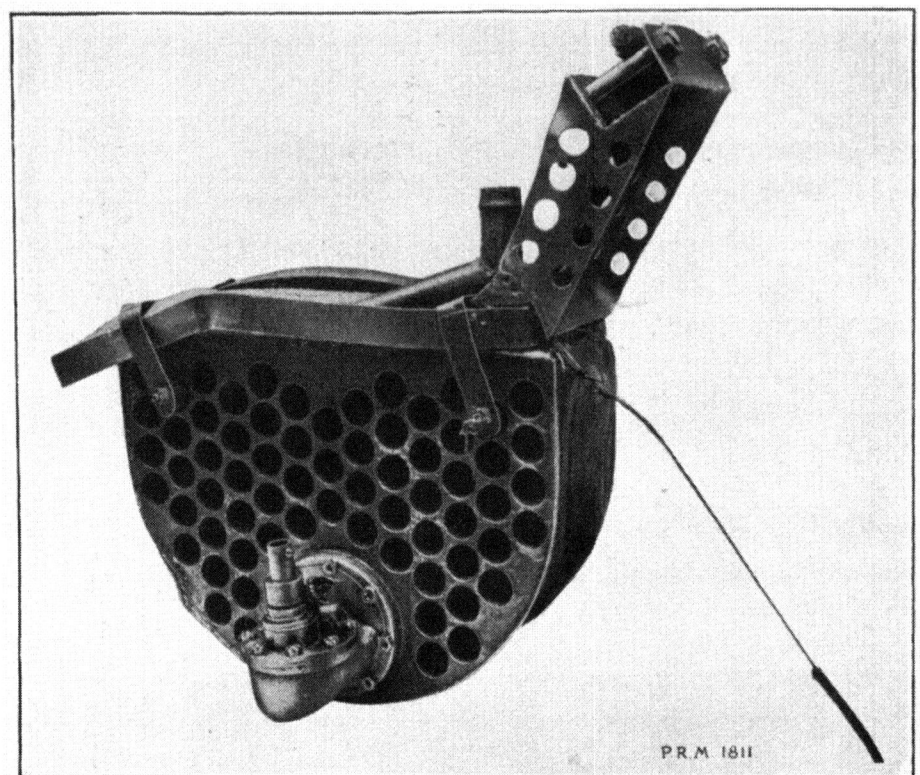

Fig. 71.

Five-engined Giant. Oil Radiator and Gear Pump.

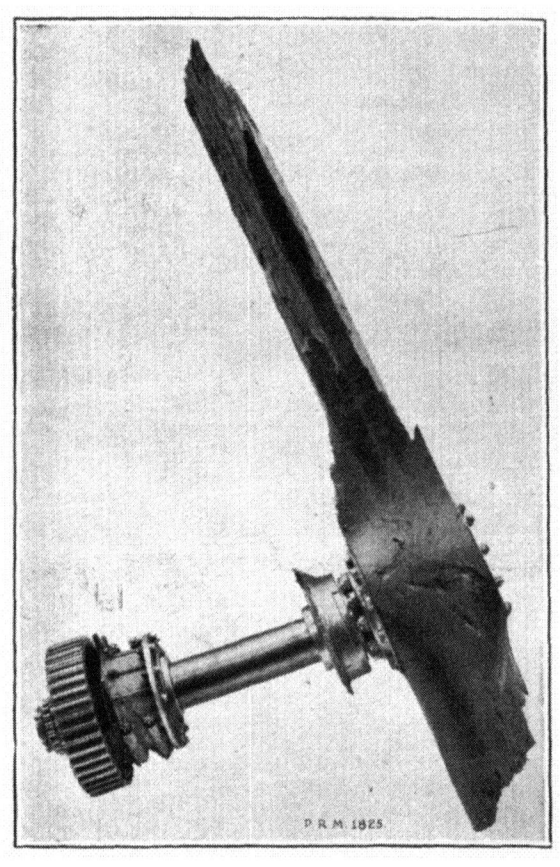

Fig. 72.

Five-engined Giant. Pusher Screw and Driven Pinion.

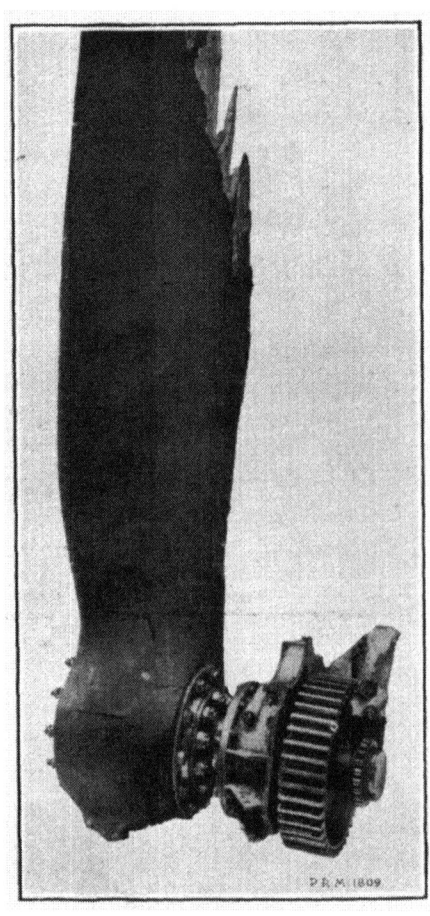

Fig. 73.

Five-engined Giant. Tractor Screw and Pinion.

Fig. 74.
Five-engined Giant. Oil Filter of Gear Box.

Fig. 75.
Five-engined Giant. Engine Control Levers.

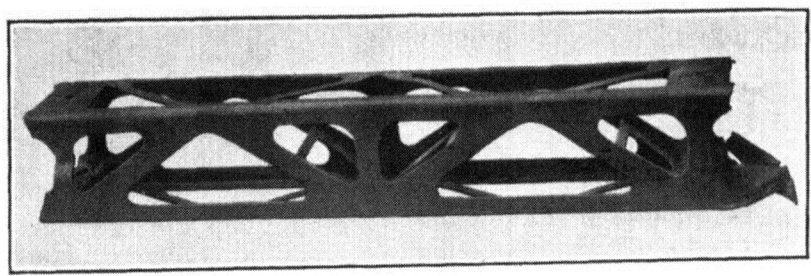

Fig. 76.
Five-engined Giant. Engine Bearer Transverse Girder.

Fig. 77.
Five-engined Giant. "Douglas" Type Wireless and Heating Generator.

Fig. 78.
Five-engined Giant. Pump and Transformer.

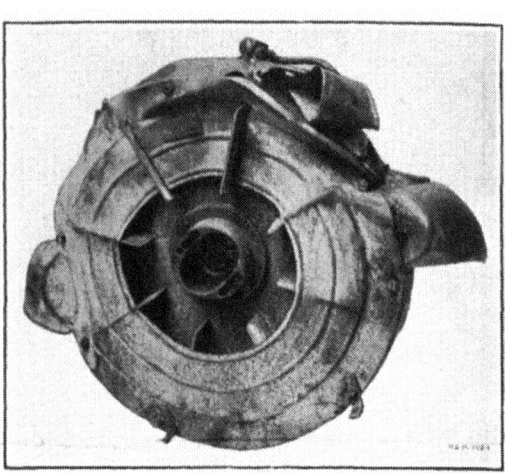

Fig. 79.
Five-engined Giant. Rear View of Engine and Flywheel.

Fig. 80.
Five-engined Giant. Wireless Generator.

Fig. 81.
Five-engined Giant. Cowling and Dynamo Drive.

Fig. 82.
Twin-engined Gotha. Front of Fuselage.
Note Morell Anemometer Air Speed Indicator.

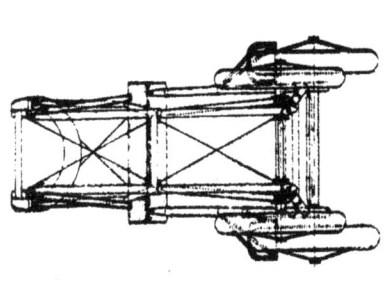
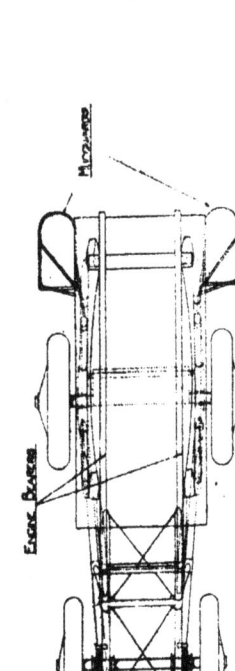

GOTHA TWIN ENGINE BIPLANE

ASSEMBLY OF UNDERCARRIAGE

DRG. N° A D 2048.

ISSUED BY T.7. AIR BOARD OFFICE

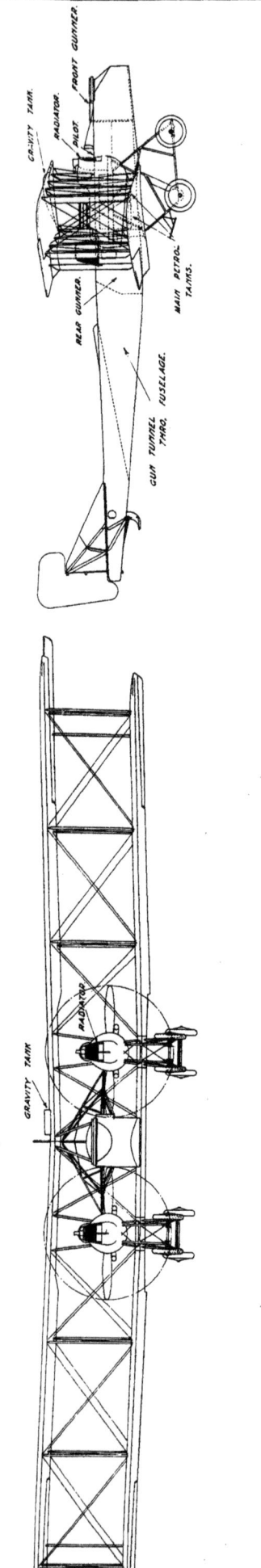

GOTHA.
TWIN-ENGINE-BIPLANE.
TYPE-GO-G5.

Scale ⅛" = 1 FOOT

GENERAL - PARTICULARS.

SPAN-(TOP PLANE)-OVER-TIPS-OF-AILERONS.	77'-0"
" (BTM ")	71'-9"
GAP.	7'-0"
CHORD.	7'-2½" to 7'-6"
TAIL-PLANE-SPAN.	13'-6"
OVERALL-LENGTH.	4'-0"
ENGINE-CENTRES.	14'-0"
ENGINES-(MERCEDES)	260 H.P. EACH.
SET-BACK-OF-PLANES.	4".
PROPELLER-(DIA.)	10'-2".
CENTRES-OF-UNDERCARRIAGE-WHEELS.	2'-7½ & 3'-2⅜"

www.ingramcontent.com/pod-product-compliance
Ingram Content Group UK Ltd.
Pitfield, Milton Keynes, MK11 3LW, UK
UKHW051525180426
11947UKWH00019B/1584